Jesus the Hero

Reading the Bible as Literature

How Bible Stories Work: A Guided Study of Biblical Narrative

Sweeter Than Honey, Richer Than Gold: A Guided Study of Biblical Poetry

Letters of Grace & Beauty: A Guided Literary Study of New Testament Epistles

Jesus the Hero: A Guided Literary Study of the Gospels

Symbols & Reality: A Guided Study of Prophecy, Apocalypse, and Visionary Literature

Short Sentences Long Remembered: A Guided Study of Proverbs and Other Wisdom Literature

Jesus the Hero

A GUIDED LITERARY STUDY
OF THE GOSPELS

LELAND RYKEN

LEXHAM PRESS

Contents

Series Preface

This series is part of the mission of the publisher to equip Christians to understand and teach the Bible effectively by giving them reliable tools for handling the biblical text. Within that landscape, the niche that my volumes are designed to fill is the literary approach to the Bible. This has been my scholarly passion for nearly half a century. It is my belief that a literary approach to the Bible is the common reader's friend, in contrast to more specialized types of scholarship on the Bible.

Nonetheless, the literary approach to the Bible needs to be defended against legitimate fears by evangelical Christians, and through the years I have not scorned to clear the territory of misconceptions as part of my defense of a literary analysis of the Bible. In kernel form, my message has been this:

1. To view the Bible as literature is not a suspect modern idea, nor does it need to imply theological liberalism. The idea of the Bible as literature began with the writers of the Bible, who display literary qualities in their writings and who refer with technical precision to a wide range of literary genres such as psalm, proverb, parable, apocalypse, and many more.

2. Although fiction is a common trait of literature, it is not an essential feature of it. A work of literature can be replete with literary technique and artifice while remaining historically factual.

3. To approach the Bible as literature need not be characterized by viewing the Bible *only* as literature, any more than reading it as history requires us to see only the history of the Bible.

4. When we see literary qualities in the Bible we are not attempting to bring the Bible down to the level of ordinary literature; it is simply an objective statement about the inherent nature of the Bible. The Bible can be trusted to reveal its extraordinary qualities if we approach it with ordinary methods of literary analysis.

To sum up, it would be tragic if we allowed ourselves to be deprived of literary methods of analyzing the Bible by claims that are fallacies.

What, then, does it mean to approach the Bible as literature? A literary study of the Bible should begin where any other approach begins—by accepting as true all that the biblical writers claim about their book. These claims include its inspiration and superintendence by God, its infallibility, its historical truthfulness, its unique power to infiltrate people's lives, and its supreme authority.

With that as a foundation, a literary approach to the Bible is characterized by the following traits:

1. An acknowledgment that the Bible comes to us in a predominantly literary format. In the words of C. S. Lewis, "There is a . . . sense in which the Bible, since it is after all literature, cannot properly be read except as literature; and the different parts of it as the different sorts

of literature they are."[1] The overall format of the Bible is that of an anthology of literature.

2. In keeping with that, a literary approach identifies the genres and other literary forms of the Bible and analyzes individual texts in keeping with those forms. An awareness of literary genres and forms programs how we analyze a biblical text and opens doors into a text that would otherwise remain closed.

3. A literary approach begins with the premise that a work of literature embodies universal human experience. Such truthfulness to human experience is complementary to the tendency of traditional approaches to the Bible to mainly see ideas in it. A literary approach corrects a commonly held fallacy that the Bible is a theology book with proof texts attached.

4. A literary approach to the Bible is ready to grant value to the biblical authors' skill with language and literary technique, seeing these as an added avenue to our enjoyment of the Bible.

5. A literary approach to the Bible takes its humble place alongside the two other main approaches—the theological and the historical. These three domains are established by the biblical writers themselves, who usually combine all three elements in their writings. However, in terms of space, the Bible is a predominantly literary book. Usually the historical and theological material is packaged in literary form.

These traits and methods of literary analysis govern the content of my series of guided studies to the genres of the Bible.

Although individual books in my series are organized by the leading literary genres that appear in the Bible, I need to highlight

---

1   *Reflections on the Psalms* (New York: Harcourt, Brace & World, 1958), 3.

that all of these genres have certain traits in common. Literature itself, en masse, makes up a homogenous whole. In fact, we can speak of *literature as a genre* (the title of the opening chapter of a book titled *Kinds of Literature*). The traits that make up literature as a genre will simply be assumed in the volumes in this series. They include the following: universal, recognizable human experience concretely embodied as the subject matter; the packaging of this subject matter in distinctly literary genres; the authors' use of special resources of language that set their writing apart from everyday expository discourse; stylistic excellence and other forms of artistry that are part of the beauty of a work of literature.

What are the advantages that come from applying the methods of literary analysis? In brief, they are as follows: an improved method of interacting with biblical texts in terms of the type of writing that they are; doing justice to the specificity of texts (again because the approach is tailored to the genres of a text); ability to see unifying patterns in a text; relating texts to everyday human experience; enjoyment of the artistic skill of biblical authors.

Summary

A book needs to be read in keeping with its author's intention. We can see from the Bible itself that it is a thoroughly literary book. God superintended its authors to write a very (though not wholly) literary book. To pay adequate attention to the literary qualities of the Bible not only helps to unlock the meanings of the Bible; it is also a way of honoring the literary intentions of its authors. Surely biblical authors regarded everything that they put into their writing as important. We also need to regard those things as important.

Introduction

What You Need to Know
about the Gospels

The Gospels are surrounded by such a cloud of conflicting claims that it is best to begin with a brief section of "frequently asked questions" that will clarify the premises that underlie this guided study.

- *What is a Gospel?* In common usage, the word "gospel" names the genre of the first four books of the New Testament canon—Matthew, Mark, Luke, and John.
- *What is the origin of this label?* Originally the word "gospel" denoted not a type of writing but the message about the life and teachings of Jesus. At the start of it all is the Greek word (*euangelion*) that means "good message" (Latinized version, *evangelium*). The Old English word-for-word translation of that was *god-spell*, meaning "good news" or "glad tidings." The word was quickly extended to the four books of the New Testament that tell about the life and

teachings of Jesus.

- *Who wrote the Gospels?* The Gospels are eyewitness accounts of the life of Jesus. The authors, known to posterity as "the evangelists," were either disciples of Jesus who accompanied him during his years of public ministry or associates of the disciples who drew upon eyewitness accounts. The writers of the Gospels were designated by Jesus to be the authorized recorders of his life and ministry (John 14:26). It seems plausible that in compiling their books under God's superintendence they used what we call *historical sources,* ultimately of eyewitnesses. First John 1:1–3 gives a picture of what it was like to be an eyewitness of Jesus' life.
- *When were the Gospels written?* The Gospels were written in the decades immediately following the death and resurrection of Jesus.

This guide takes a literary approach to the Gospels that focuses on the forms in which the content of the four books is embodied. It is possible for readers who do not accept all of the premises stated above to meet on common ground in appropriating the analytic methods of this guide.

A Unique Genre

The only anthology in which the table of contents includes the category of gospel is the New Testament. This is a tip-off that the Gospels are a unique genre. The writers of the Gospels produced a new literary form to express the truth about a unique person and message. The world-changing events surrounding Jesus generated their own genre.

Nonetheless, the common claim that the Gospel is a unique genre has produced misconceptions. We should note the following two points in particular. First, the uniqueness of the Gospels has more to do with their content than the forms in which that content is presented. The characterization of the protagonist (Jesus) and his message are chiefly what makes the Gospels unique.

Second, while the books that we know as the Gospels have no exact parallel in other literature, the individual genres that appear in the Gospels—story, parable, discourse, dialogue, biography, and so forth—are familiar. The blanket claim that the Gospels are unique has had the unfortunate effect of leading readers to ignore the ways in which ordinary rules of reading and interpretation apply to the Gospels. In their individual parts, the Gospels are often similar to familiar literature.

On the side of literary form, what is unique about the Gospels is not primarily the individual units or genres but the way in which the writers brought these together into a composite whole. The Gospels are hybrid books and mixed-genre books. They are collections of diverse material, similar to books that we know as anthologies. It is easy to see how the material with which the writers worked produced such a form. The individual units of discourse, dialogue, and narrative were collected piecemeal by the writers. It is a common assumption that parts of the Gospels circulated orally before being written down in a composite form.

Misconceptions and Their Antidotes

The Gospels are difficult books. Faced with the difficulties, interpreters have come up with false claims about them. In the rest of this unit of the chapter, I will name some common misconceptions of the Gospels. I will assert that these viewpoints are inaccurate statements and are *not* true of the Gospels, with each one accompanied by a counterclaim that *is* true of them.

The primary form of the Gospels is not the sermon or saying. The view of the Gospels that stood in the way of a literary approach to them for a very long time is that their original form was the sayings of Jesus and the preaching of the apostles. The point of origin for the content that eventually made up the Gospels is a matter of pure speculation. It is at least as likely that the facts of Jesus' life and teachings first circulated as stories. But regardless of how the eventual Gospels originated, their final written form is not a series of sermons or a collection of proverbs (even though these appear in the Gospels).

The primary form of the Gospels is story, or narrative. We immediately need to make the concession that approximately half of the Gospels is discourse material (some of which takes the form of dialogues between Jesus and others, to which must be added the parables of Jesus). But the context within which the discourses exist is the overall story of Jesus' life during his public years. We experience even the discourses as contributions to the overall story of Jesus.

The Gospels do not follow a strict chronological format. We are so accustomed to biographies and historical narratives being organized as a chronological sequence that we tend to assume the same of the Gospels. But the writers of the Gospels make no claim to be writing a chronologically precise narrative, so we should not make the unwarranted assumption that they did. If we look at the Gospels themselves, we find that the writers often clustered their material topically—a section of parables, for example, or a section of discourses, or a collection of conflict stories or miracle stories (arrangement by genre).

At most we can say that the Gospels are structured on a *loosely* chronological principle. They begin with the birth of Jesus or the outset of his public years of ministry. They all end with events surrounding the trial, death, and resurrection of Jesus. Within that framework, the arrangement is discontinuous and frequently non-chronological.

The Gospels are not structured as a smooth narrative flow. The novels and short stories with which we are familiar are based on the premise of a continuous narrative flow. They are constructed around a central plot conflict that runs its course and finds resolution at the end. The sequence is a cause-effect chain of events in which one main action produces the next one, which produces the next one.

By contrast, the Gospels fall into a story type known as an *episodic plot*. They are collections of stories instead of a single action. The protagonist (Jesus) remains constant from beginning to end, but the individual units (both narrative and discourse) are self-contained. Many of the secondary characters play their part and then drop out of the action. The heavy incidence of non-narrative material makes this kaleidoscopic effect even more pronounced. The formula "now for something completely different" is continuously operative. While this is not the most customary format for a book, it is the form that perfectly captures the nature of Jesus' life as a traveling teacher and miracle worker.

The Gospels are not easy to understand. Because the Gospels are relatively brief and familiar to us, the feeling can settle in that we *should* find them easy to read. After all, the Gospels seem to be straightforward and simple, as seen even in their prevailing prose style. The misconception that I need to challenge is that we should feel guilty if we find ourselves mystified as we read the Gospels.

I will speak personally in saying that for me the Gospels are a genre of "loose ends" and mysterious statements. It is a rare session of devotional reading in the Gospels that does not leave me perplexed at one point or another. I regularly find myself consulting the notes of a study Bible as I read the Gospels. Biblical scholars have multiplied subtle connections between units of the Gospels that I myself would never think of (and of which I often remain skeptical). I do not share my experience to encourage giving up on the Gospels but for the opposite reason—to suggest that the Gospels can be fully instructive and rewarding to us even when many things remain mysterious or initially elusive.

The Unity of the Gospels

The foregoing module has painted a picture of the Gospels as a disjointed collection of diverse material. Unless we can produce a counter movement toward unity, we will experience the Gospels as a bewildering collection of unrelated fragments. Fortunately, there are unifying principles that can make the Gospels manageable.

First, the Gospels have a unifying central character and hero. Everything revolves around Jesus. Most of the events, all of the discourses, and all of the dialogues involve this central character. At virtually any point in the Gospels, we are learning about the person, work, and message of Jesus. It is possible to view the Gospels as a series of concentric rings with Jesus in the center, surrounded by his closest associates the disciples, then around them the hostile religious establishment most often represented as the Pharisees, and on the periphery a crowd of onlookers and seekers (sometimes represented by a single figure who encounters Jesus).

We noted earlier that the Gospels have an episodic plot instead of a single-action plot, but the way in which Jesus is situated as the central character in all of the episodes requires us to adjust that picture. There is not a unity of *action*, but there is a unity of *hero*. Furthermore, because Jesus acts and speaks in such a way as to encounter people and demand that they make a choice for or against him, something like a unified plot conflict emerges as the Gospels unfold. It is a conflict between belief and unbelief, following Jesus and rejecting him, being saved and being lost.

The next unifying framework falls into the category of "take it or leave it," depending on whether or not you find it helpful in organizing the Gospels. If we view the composition of the Gospels from a human perspective, we can infer that the writers relied on the memories of eyewitnesses (sometimes the writers themselves). How does the memory recall events? It recalls broad outlines; it remembers single incidents; and it strings together certain sequences of events. This is what we find in the Gospels, with the process of memory as we ourselves know it helping us bring a type of unity to our experience of the Gospels.

The presence of Jesus is the "constant" in the Gospels, but with that as a foundation, we can see that the material falls into the further framework, as follows:

- the discourses and parables of Jesus: what Jesus taught
- stories involving Jesus: what Jesus did
- responses to Jesus: what Jesus elicited

That framework enables the material to fall into place.

Finally, the presence of *archetypes* allows the Gospels to emerge in our minds as unified compositions. Archetypes are the master images of the imagination, and their differentiating trait is that they are *recurrent* in literature and life. They fall into three categories—plot motifs (such as the journey and test), character types (such as the hero and martyr), and images/settings/places (such as the valley and court). Archetypes keep appearing in the Gospels and become a unifying element. The following is a random collection of specimens, by no means exhaustive but serving the purpose of providing some illustrations: hero, journey, conflict, refuser of festivities, sea, night, mountain, loyal follower, enemy, martyr, traitor, village, miracle, conversion, and encounter. We keep encountering archetypes like these as we read the Gospels, and their presence becomes a unifying element in our experience of the Gospels.

Tips for Reading and Teaching the Gospels

The following list of suggestions is slanted in the direction of a literary reading of the Gospels, but some of the items are simply good general methods for interacting with the material, not based on literary assumptions:

- It is crucial to focus on the unit that is before you and not strain to fit it into a larger framework. If it is important to connect a unit to something else, you can trust your intuition to see that connection. Your first responsibility is to the unit before you. A more technical way to say this is that we must avoid escaping from the text to its context. Biblical scholarship took a wrong turn when scholars became more interested in context than text.

- Every unit, regardless of its specific genre, contributes to our understanding of Jesus—his person, his mission, his teaching. The Gospels are our great "primary source" on Jesus. It is therefore always important to ask what we learn about Jesus in a given passage.

- The entire remainder of this guide will be based on the premise that specific genres make up the Gospels. To anticipate a point that will be clarified in the subsequent chapters, it is crucial to analyze a given unit in keeping with the dynamics of the genre of that unit. A conflict story requires different analytic considerations than a discourse does.

- The overall genre that governs the Gospels is narrative, or story. The familiar considerations of story need to be a constant frame of reference for us as we read and teach—a storyline, a protagonist or central character, a cast of additional characters, a setting in which the action occurs, dialogue as a potential vehicle for the action, and so forth. Even the discourses of Jesus are placed into a narrative context and contribute to the ongoing story. The practice of "thinking story" as we read the Gospels will not let us down.

• The unifying elements noted in the preceding module are continuously helpful as we read or teach the Gospels.

Some Useful Parallels That Illuminate the Gospels

Over the course of my career of teaching the Gospels, I have encountered some unconventional ways of viewing the Gospels that solve a lot of interpretive problems for me. As I have analyzed these frameworks, it is obvious that the Gospels are mainly *analogies* to the genres that I am about to share.

Television documentary. What I have called a television documentary is also familiar to us through documentary videos used in high school and college classrooms. What things make up a television documentary of a famous leader? Consider the following: a script of basic information that provides a skeleton for the video; a narrator who ties the individual fragments together and provides transitions between them; photographs that document various stages and events in the subject's life; video clips of landmark addresses, interviews, and events in the life of the featured person; and interviews of other people as they comment on the subject of the documentary. There are crowd scenes, scenes of the subject with an inner circle, and scenes of the subject in solitude. These same ingredients converge in the Gospels. The Gospels are obviously not television documentaries, but if we have the genre of the television documentary in our thinking, the Gospels will seem familiar to us.

The television sports replay. This genre is best represented by television coverage of a football game. Key plays in a football game are subjected to a dazzling array of technical feats by the television crew, including the same play from multiple camera angles, slow-motion replay, close-up, wide-angle, forward-and-reverse, and split-screen. These are sometimes accompanied by verbal commentary from an expert.

What is the relevance of this to the Gospels? It sheds light on the so-called synoptic problem—the presence of slightly divergent but similar material in two or more of the Gospels. People of liberal persuasion claim that this is evidence that the Gospels are not reliable, but the sports replay shows us that a single event can be accurately viewed from multiple perspectives.

The political campaign. The institution of a politician on the campaign trail also provides a helpful perspective on the synoptic situation. Politicians on the campaign trail reenact a basic paradigm many times over, but the details vary slightly at virtually every stop on a day's travels. Politicians state their views over and over, but not usually in verbatim form. Nearly identical events occur—the arrival of the caravan or airplane, the interaction of the politician with people lining the way, visiting a local company or landmark, and leave-taking. The basic ingredients are *nearly* identical, but not totally identical. Surely this analogy provides a common-sense solution to many of the alleged discrepancies among the Gospels. We cannot remind ourselves too often that Jesus was a *traveling* teacher and miracle worker. Certain basic situations kept getting reenacted in slightly different forms.

Mosaic and collage. Mosaics and collages bring a collection of discrete but related fragments together in such a way as to produce a composite picture of a given subject. The Gospels are individual collections of material about Jesus. They are not a continuous narrative, but all of the details fit together to form a composite and ultimately unified mosaic or collage.

Summary

The foregoing discussion illuminates the paradoxical nature of the Gospels. The Gospels invite us into them with a *surface simplicity.* They are prose biographies that have a single purpose—to tell us the facts about Jesus' life and mission, with a view of instilling belief in Jesus as Savior. All of this seems simple.

But there are equally strong elements working toward complexity. The Gospels do not tell just one story but many individual ones. The overriding genre is narrative, but half of the material is discourse. The Gospels are an anthology of a dozen or more individual genres (as later chapters in this guide will show). The prose style is usually (but not always) simple, but figurative language and mystery abound.

Narrative Genre

The Primary Form

When we speak of narrative, or story, as the primary form of the Gospels, we have two dimensions in view. One is the overview of each Gospel as a book. While this narrative superstructure, or umbrella, for each book does not yield a methodology for interacting with individual passages, it is useful information to have at our disposal as we interact with individual units, which always contribute to an overall story. The other dimension is that we need to assimilate individual stories in the Gospels by using the usual tools of narrative analysis. The next module of this chapter will elaborate on that.

The Narrative Nature of the Gospels

Even though we do not read or teach the Gospels in a single session, it is important that we sometimes take an overview of them as a book. A book has a beginning, middle, and end. In the Gospels, this takes a narrative form. The Gospels do not have a thesis and subordinate points the way an informational book does. Instead, they tell the story of Jesus' life and ministry.

The beginning is Jesus' birth and his initiation of his three-year public life. After that we accompany Jesus during his ministry as a traveling teacher and miracle worker. At the end, the Gospel writers devote a substantial segment of their account to the events surrounding Jesus' last weeks on earth.

This does not mean that the entire middle of the Gospels consists of events. Nearly as much space is devoted to Jesus' discourses and teaching (including dialogues and parables) as to stories that recount what he did. Nonetheless, all of the material fits into the general flow of the story of Jesus. What are the implications?

First, things fall into place if we operate with an awareness that stories consist of three main elements—action or plot, characters, and settings. A plot always has a *protagonist,* a word based on a Greek word that carries the meaning of "first struggler." It is useful to think of Jesus as protagonist of the individual Gospels. We go through the action as the observant traveling companion of this "first struggler."

Additionally, plots are constructed on the principle of conflict. In the Gospels, various individuals and groups oppose Jesus, and this adds up to an overall conflict between good and evil, belief and unbelief, submission to Jesus and hardness of heart toward him.

Stories always have a cast of characters, and it is useful to think of the Gospels in this way. The cast of characters represents a cross-section of humanity, not only in Jesus' day but in all places and times. These characters often become our representatives, with the result that we can see ourselves and our acquaintances in them and in their choices for or against Jesus. It is no distortion to say that as we read the Gospels we do not primarily encounter a set of ideas but rather a memorable gallery of people.

We also experience the Gospels as an ever-changing series of places. Specific geographical places figure prominently in the Gospels and are part of the evidential or circumstantial reality of them. The Gospels are situated in real life, not a fictional world. This sense of reality is heightened by the high degree to which the Gospels root us in a world of elemental nature—mountain, sea, heat, pathway, plain, village, and such like. Geography often assumes a symbolic function in the Gospels, with Jerusalem (for example) symbolizing rejection of Jesus by the religious authorities and the countryside often being a place of conversion and discipleship.

The Narrative Units within the Gospels

The second importance of narrative as the primary form of the Gospels is that we need to apply the ordinary rules of narrative analysis whenever we come upon narrative units as we read the Gospels. Before we explore that in detail, we need to pause to note that the stories in the Gospels exist on a literary continuum.

At one end of the continuum is a barebones account of what happened, devoid of any embellishment or filling out of details. It is a summary of action and no more. It serves the documentary function of recording facts, much as a newspaper account does. Literary scholars and teachers of writing call this *expository writing* (informational or explanatory writing). There are many documentary, or expository, narrative fragments of the following type in the Gospels:

> The Spirit immediately drove him out into the wilderness. And he was in the wilderness forty days, being tempted by Satan. And he was with the wild animals, and the angels were ministering to him. (Mark 1:12–13)

The usual narrative ingredients are present. Accordingly, the right terms to use when analyzing the passage are protagonist, antagonist, additional characters or agents, plot conflict, and setting. These elements, though, appear in such abbreviated form that there is little analysis that can be done with them.

As we move across the continuum, stories are told in greater detail. At the far end we have full-fledged literary narrative. In the background is the fact that literature is a presentation of human experience rendered as concretely as possible and in such a way as to allow us to relive the story in our imagination. The rest of this chapter will discuss how to read and analyze the literary narratives that we encounter in the Gospels, in the form of a primer or summary of "first things" in regard to the stories within the Gospels.

Literary Narratives within the Gospels

There is no prescribed order in which to analyze a literary narrative. In fact, if the story is told at such length that we can break it down into successive scenes or episodes, we might want to deal with plot, setting, and characterization in each unit, and then move to the next unit and do everything that the unit requires before moving on. But it is also possible to examine even a multi-episode story as a whole, dealing with the various elements one at a time.

Somewhat arbitrarily, then, I will start with plot. The plot of a story is the main action. While a long narrative like a novel or play might have multiple plot lines, this is unlikely in the concentrated stories in the Gospels. The first thing to identify in a Gospel story is thus the unifying action. For example, in the story of Jesus and the woman at the well (John 4:1–42), the unifying action is Jesus' quest to bring the woman to salvation. It is also in the nature of plot to be constructed around one or more plot conflicts, and it is essential to name them. This requires analysis, but it pays big dividends in our understanding of a story.

Once we have identified the central action and one or more plot conflicts, we need to divide the story into its successive phases.

These can be called *episodes, units,* or *scenes* (with the latter based on the model of a drama or play). Then we need to label these units in such a way as to keep the central action and conflict in view. It is also useful to keep the paradigm of beginning-middle-end in mind. The purpose of dividing a story into its successive phases is that it allows us to trace the development of the initial situation step by step to its conclusion. Most stories are based on the premise of an initial problem that gradually moves toward a solution.

Setting is the neglected element in most people's experience of stories, and that is a great loss because setting plays a crucial role in stories. We need to start at an observational level by identifying the place in which an action occurs and noting the literal, physical properties of the place. Sometimes even a relatively short narrative might have multiple settings. For example, the five-verse story of Jesus' calling of Levi, or Matthew (Matt. 9:9–13), begins at seaside, then shifts to Matthew's tax booth on the side of the road, and ends at a dinner scene inside Matthew's house.

Having identified the facts of the setting, we can usually move toward analysis of those facts. For example, the most frequent function of a setting is that it *enables* the action that occurs within it. Identifying this link or correspondence between setting and action yields a lot. Additionally, settings often take on symbolic overtones, and we can identify these as well.

The story of Jesus' healing of blind Bartimaeus (Mark 10: 46–52) affords an illustration. The account begins with a crowd scene that includes Jesus, his disciples, and "a great crowd" leaving Jericho. The Gospels are travel stories, and one of the most common settings is the road, which is the enabling element for many events. This is what happens in the story of the healing of Bartimaeus, who is at the roadside when Jesus encounters him and heals him. At the end we read that Bartimaeus "followed him on the way."

The continuous picture of people being on the road with Jesus epitomizes Jesus' life and takes on a symbolic meaning as well. To be on the road with Jesus is to follow him.

Characters are the third constant element in a story. The techniques by which storytellers create or present characters is called *characterization.* Before we examine how authors conduct characterization, we should take time to state the goal of character analysis.

The primary goal is simply to get to know the characters in a story as fully as the details in the story allow. Once we have codified what a character is like, we need to analyze the function or role of that character in the story. Much of what a storyteller wishes us to understand about life is embodied in the characters. The theme of a story often resides in the example that the storyteller puts before us to imitate or reject, and often the example is a character.

Here is a brief checklist to apply for analyzing the characters in a Gospel narrative:

1. It is always useful to begin by assembling the cast of characters.
2. In this cast of characters, who are the protagonist, the antagonist(s), additional characters of primary importance (if any), and the minor characters who are present mainly to fill a specific function (such as onlooker to the action)?
3. For the major characters, we need to compile as complete a portrait as the details allow: traits, roles, relationships, external actions and internal ones (thoughts and feelings), and such like. Anything that helps us know a character is relevant.
4. We need to reach conclusions about the function of a character in the story, including what we learn about life from a given character.

5. Finally, the ingredients of a story (plot, setting, character) work together to embody one or more themes (generalizations about life). A good working premise is that every story is at some level an example story, so we can always ask what the story is an example *of.* In performing this exercise, we need to be aware that storytellers put two types of examples before us—positive ones to follow and negative ones to avoid.

A Specimen Gospel Story

The story of Jesus' stilling of the storm narrated in Mark 4:35–41 will enable us to see all that has been said above in a mere seven verses. Here is the text:

> [35]On that day, when evening had come, he said to them, "Let us go across to the other side." [36]And leaving the crowd, they took him with them in the boat, just as he was. And other boats were with him. [37]And a great windstorm arose, and the waves were breaking into the boat, so that the boat was already filling. [38]But he was in the stern, asleep on the cushion. And they woke him and said to him, "Teacher, do you not care that we are perishing?" [39]And he awoke and rebuked the wind and said to the sea, "Peace! Be still!" And the wind ceased, and there was a great calm. [40]He said to them, "Why are you so afraid? Have you still no faith?" [41]And they were filled with great fear and said to one another, "Who then is this, that even the wind and the sea obey him?"

Our starting premise is that a story is designed to get us to relive an event as fully as the details allow. The power of narrative is that it puts us into the middle of a situation and series of events. As readers we need to be active in visualizing and hearing as much as possible. With that as an assumed framework, the following is a very brief application of the narrative checklist presented above:

- *Setting:* a small boat on a sea notorious for sudden and violent storms; nighttime darkness; an atmosphere of danger and vulnerability; a scene of desperation as waves start to sink the boat. Contribution to the story: it enables the testing of the disciples that is the mainspring of the action.

- *Characters:* the disciples are the protagonists (not to be equated with heroes) with whom we go through the central action; Jesus is the master of the situation and a foil to the disciples. Ruling traits: the disciples' fear and Jesus' calmness; also the human weakness of the disciples and the divine power of Jesus.

- *Plot or action:* more complex than analysis of setting and character. Analysis begins by dividing the story into successive units and labeling each one. I call this "identifying the action," and I have found in half a century of teaching literature that it always yields dividends for later analysis to take the time to identify the action. The first dividend is that it imposes a unity on the story. For the story of the calming of the sea, the action unfolds in these phases: departure from the safe land to the scene of danger and testing (vv. 35–36); the crisis of the storm (vv. 37–38); solving the crisis with a miracle (v. 39); Jesus' response and verdict (v. 40); the disciples' response and verdict (v. 41). After determining the sequential structure of the story, we need to identify the unifying action and plot conflicts. The unifying action is the testing of the disciples' faith. At the physical level, the plot conflict is between the disciples and the storm that threatens their lives. That generates a personal conflict between the disciples and Jesus. At a more interpretive level, the questions that Jesus asks in verse 40 ("Why are you so afraid? Have you still no faith?") confirm a conflict that we can infer from earlier details between fear and faith on the part of the disciples.

- *Themes or controlling ideas:* the divine power of Jesus to rescue people and the need for people to trust in him.

LEARNING BY DOING

Before applying what this chapter has covered, you should review the chapter and draw up your own working list of activities that need to be done when mastering and teaching a story in the Gospels. Then apply your list to the following story:

Then they seized him and led him away, bringing him into the high priest's house, and Peter was following at a distance. And when they had kindled a fire in the middle of the courtyard and sat down together, Peter sat down among them. Then a servant girl, seeing him as he sat in the light and looking closely at him, said, "This man also was with him." But he denied it, saying, "Woman, I do not know him." And a little later someone else saw him and said, "You also are one of them." But Peter said, "Man, I am not." And after an interval of about an hour still another insisted, saying, "Certainly this man also was with him, for he too is a Galilean." But Peter said, "Man, I do not know what you are talking about." And immediately, while he was still speaking, the rooster crowed. And the Lord turned and looked at Peter. And Peter remembered the saying of the Lord, how he had said to him, "Before the rooster crows today, you will deny me three times." And he went out and wept bitterly. (Luke 22:54–62)

Biography and Hero Story

We need to begin with three foundational principles. First, the entire content of the Gospels is biographical (an adjective) in the sense of recording accurate information about Jesus.

Second, it is unnecessary and unfruitful to spend time searching for biographical models in the first-century classical world. Biographers do not sit down and ask, What model do I wish to follow? They begin with a passion to acquaint readers with the subject of their biography, and then generate whatever forms are required to accomplish that task.

Third, we need to cast aside all thoughts that a hero story needs to be fictional. Most of the hero stories that we read and hear are fictional, but not all of them. A hero story belongs to that category because the narrative, whether fictional or factual, adheres to the rules of a hero story.

Differentiating between Biography and Hero Story

A biography is a non-fictional, factual record of a person's life. We have inaccurately been told that a biography needs to possess certain formal characteristics. There is no prescribed format or content for a biography. To prove that assertion, all we need to do is read a range of biographies. The only "constant" in a biography is that everything included in it acquaints a reader with the subject of the biography. The Gospels in their totality meet that criterion. While this makes them *biographical,* certain formal characteristics kick in that make some of the Gospel material literary in a way that a *biography* is not.

What, then, is a hero story? When we use the word "story," we imply that the narrative meets the criterion of being literary rather than expository (informational). A story consists of the elements discussed in the preceding chapter, including the following: a plot that can be arranged into a sequence of linked episodes or scenes; a unifying action possessing the pattern of beginning-middle-end; one or more plot conflicts that move to a resolution; one or more settings in which the action occurs; a cast of characters, including a protagonist with whom we go through the action and one or more antagonists arrayed against him or her. In addition, a literary narrative exhibits literary features such as stylistic interest, dialogue, and dramatic irony. Finally, literature embodies human experience as concretely as possible and with a certain fullness of detail.

Do biographies contain stories like that? They do not. They are packaged in the form of expository writing. Writers of biography achieve fullness of supporting data by adding more and more factual data, not with literary elements of description, characterization, and plot.

Defining the Genre of Hero Story

A hero story is a story, first of all. This means that everything covered in the preceding chapter on narrative applies to a hero story. With a hero story, we need to begin by applying the methodology of straightforward narrative analysis.

The hero story aspect is an additional layer in the story that we need to analyze. It constitutes a second round, or overlay, of considerations. Here are the additional factors that enter the picture:

- All stories are constructed around a protagonist to varying degrees, but a hero story highlights this focus on the central character. A simple rule of thumb is to consider ourselves the observant traveling companions of the hero, with a goal of getting to know that person as fully as possible.
- The protagonist of a hero story is *largely* (but usually not *wholly*) idealized (portrayed in a positive light and in such a way as to lead us to admire him or her). That is why we call the protagonist a hero.
- A hero is representative of the culture producing him or her, so that we can see universal or communal conflicts and aspirations embodied in the hero. A hero story sums up what a culture most wants to say about life and its own experience.
- Along with giving us a picture of heroic character, a hero story gives us a picture of what constitutes *heroic action*—a model of ideal action that adds up to a picture of the good life.
- A hero captures people's imaginations and serves as an inspiration.

All of these traits can be turned into a series of questions that we ask of the text. What do we know about the hero? What is admirable about this hero and worthy of emulation? How does the hero represent human longings and aspirations? In view of the hero's actions, what constitutes exemplary character and action? What captivates our imaginations and inspires us?

Even though the expository, biographical parts of the Gospels are not literary stories, the "hero" half of the equation stated above does apply to everything we find in the Gospels. The writers of the units of biography in the Gospels were not thinking in terms of the objectivity that characterizes modern biographies. Their intention was the same as the author of a hero story, namely, to record the perfection of Jesus and instill a desire to follow him and believe in him as Savior. In both the biographical and literary parts of the Gospels, Jesus is presented as the perfect hero.

An additional point needs to be tucked in: although the genre of hero story is a narrative form, there is a sense in which the hero of the Gospels is known to us as much by what he says and teaches as by what he does. It is therefore appropriate to include the discourses of Jesus as part of the overall picture of Jesus as hero. The discourses are an important part of what we know about Jesus as hero.

Biography in the Gospels

This module will explore the units in the Gospels that fall into the genre of biography, and the next module will cover the more literary units that place themselves into the category of hero story. Both biography and hero story aim to tell the truth about Jesus, and in that sense both genres are "documentary" in nature.

Before we explore a specimen unit of biography, we need to revisit the distinction between expository writing and literary writing. In college writing courses and literature courses, it is customary to make a distinction between *telling* and *showing*. To "tell" means to summarize, to state things abstractly, to offer an interpretation or commentary on a body of data. To "show" means to embody, to enact, to present, to re-create an event in sufficient detail and concretion to enable readers to relive the event in their imaginations. Applied to the Gospels, a passage of biography informs us about *what* happened but does not delineate *how* it happened, whereas a hero story lets us know *how* an event unfolded and ended.

Here is a specimen of biography from the Gospels:

> When they had crossed over, they came to land at Gennesaret and moored to the shore. And when they got out of the boat, the people immediately recognized him and ran about the whole region and began to bring the sick people on their beds to wherever they heard he was. And wherever he came, in villages, cities, or countryside, they laid the sick in the marketplaces and implored him that they might touch even the fringe of his garment. And as many as touched it were made well. (Mark 6:53–56)

This is a summary, not an enactment. It compresses information about events covering multiple days and settings into just four verses. The purpose of the passage is not to get us to relive a specific event in detail but to convey information about Jesus and his ministry. The passage would be right at home in a biography but not a literary anthology. There is no plot conflict moving to resolution, no detailed description of setting, no techniques of characterization. The passage is a summary of information.

The methodology for interacting with units of biography is exceedingly simple. The basic formula is to list what we know about Jesus on the basis of the passage; questions such as the following are an aid to achieving that goal:

- What does Jesus say or do?
- What role or roles does Jesus fill? (In this passage, miracle worker and healer.)
- How do others respond to Jesus?
- What conclusions can we reach regarding the person and work of Jesus on the basis of this data?
- With this ideal before us, how should we respond to Jesus in terms of belief, allegiance, and behavior?

There is nothing prescriptive about this list; if other questions seem useful to you, they can certainly be used.

Hero Story

By way of reminder, this chapter deals with the narrative units in the Gospels; the discourse material is not in view. In contrast to the barebones passages of biography, hero stories enact instead of summarize, and show rather than tell. We are dealing with a continuum, not an either/or situation. As we move across the continuum from biography to literary hero story, the narratives are told in greater and greater detail, and correspondingly we can perform more and more literary and narrative analysis. Here is a specimen hero story from the Gospels:

> As he drew near to Jericho, a blind man was sitting by the roadside begging. And hearing a crowd going by, he inquired what this meant. They told him, "Jesus of Nazareth is passing by." And he cried out, "Jesus, Son of David, have mercy on me!" And those who were in front rebuked him, telling him to be silent. But he cried out all the more, "Son of David, have mercy on me!" And Jesus stopped and commanded him to be brought to him. And when he came near, he asked him, "What do you want me to do for you?" He said, "Lord, let me recover my sight." And Jesus said to him, "Recover your sight; your faith has made you well." And immediately he recovered his sight and followed him, glorifying God. And all the people, when they saw it, gave praise to God. (Luke 18:35–43)

On the surface, this may seem to be similar to the unit of biography considered above, but in fact we are moving in an entirely different world. Despite its brevity, there is a relative abundance of detail, and certainly the event comes alive in our imaginations in such a way that we can relive it. A hero story is a story before it is a hero story, so we need to begin by applying the usual considerations of plot (conflict moving to resolution, or problem moving to solution), setting (the literal facts and the way in which these details contribute to the action), and characterization (seen not only in what Jesus does but also in the responses he elicits from others).

Having analyzed the story as a story, we can apply a further round of considerations relating to its status as a hero story, as follows:

- By what means does the story focus our primary attention on Jesus?
- What elements in the story elevate Jesus to a position as an ideal or exemplary hero? What is heroic about Jesus?
- How does the story encourage readers to respond to the heroic example of Jesus that the story places before us?

LEARNING BY DOING

The following two-unit passage (Mark 2:1–14) contains a hero story followed by a paragraph of "barebones" biography. This specimen passage will provide a test case for applying what this chapter has covered. As you work your way through the two paragraphs, it will be useful to review earlier parts of this chapter.

And when he returned to Capernaum after some days, it was reported that he was at home. And many were gathered together, so that there was no more room, not even at the door. And he was preaching the word to them. And they came, bringing to him a paralytic carried by four men. And when they could not get near him because of the crowd, they removed the roof above him, and when they had made an opening, they let down the bed on which the paralytic lay. And when Jesus saw their faith, he said to the paralytic, "My son, your sins are forgiven." Now some of the scribes were sitting there, questioning in their hearts, "Why does this man speak like that? He is blaspheming! Who can forgive sins but God alone?" And immediately Jesus, perceiving in his spirit that they thus questioned within themselves, said to them, "Why do you question these things in your hearts? Which is easier, to say to the paralytic, 'Your sins are forgiven,' or to say, 'Rise, take up your bed and walk'? But that you may know that the Son of Man has authority on earth to forgive sins"—he said to the paralytic—"I say to you, rise, pick up your bed, and go home." And he rose and immediately picked up his bed and went out before them all, so that they were all amazed and glorified God, saying, "We never saw anything like this!"

He went out again beside the sea, and all the crowd was coming to him, and he was teaching them. And as he passed by, he saw Levi the son of Alphaeus sitting at the tax booth, and he said to him, "Follow me." And he rose and followed him.

Birth and Childhood Stories

I need to end this chapter with an addendum. Scholars have evolved a composite paradigm for hero stories that encompasses the entire life of a hero as portrayed in literature, from birth to death or resurrection. This is an appropriate place to note that two of the Gospels include the early life of the hero Jesus. If we break the material down into subtypes, we come up with this list:

- genealogy: Matthew 1:1–17; Luke 3:23–38
- annunciation: Luke 1:26–38
- birth (also known as nativity): Matthew 1:18–2:18; Luke 2:1–21
- infancy: Luke 2:22–38
- childhood: Matthew 2:19–23; Luke 2:39–52

This list highlights a leading feature of the Gospels and foreshadows what a major part of this book will demonstrate, namely, that within the basic format of narrative, a host of narrative subtypes makes up the content of the Gospels.

Encounter Story and Conflict Story

With this chapter we begin a journey through specific narrative subtypes, or subgenres, in the Gospels. As we make a transition from the overriding genres of narrative and hero story to these more specialized genres, we can profitably note the following things. First, the taxonomy of genres that makes up the rest of this book is my own compilation. I gathered individual pieces of nomenclature from numerous sources, and in that sense my framework is derivative, but no source beyond my own writings brings all of these together in a single place.

Second, there are ways in which my taxonomy points to the uniqueness of the Gospels. For example, the individual or specific genres that come together in the Gospels do not converge in other books. Such Gospel forms as calling story and pronouncement story and witness story do not have counterparts in other anthologies. It is unusual if not unique to find as *many* diverse subtypes elsewhere as we find in the Gospels. The Gospels are mixed-genre books, and we need to get double mileage out of the word "mixed." The Gospels do not simply bring a large menu of genres into a single book, but they also mingle them together in seemingly random fashion. At this point the analogies of a mosaic and a collage are accurate descriptors of what we find in the Gospels, in as much as the forms are juxtaposed abruptly to each other.

But we need to be careful not to drive a complete wedge between the Gospels and familiar literature. There are parallels between the genres of the Gospels and those of extra-biblical literature. For example, it is unthinkable to read and interpret the Gospels without the genre of encounter story on our radar screen. By contrast, literary critics do not use that label when interacting with Homer's *Odyssey*. Yet we *could* use that category when dealing with *The Odyssey* because the protagonist Odysseus does, in fact, have many encounters on his ten-year journey from Troy to his home in Ithaca.

Encounter Story

A towering literary scholar of a bygone age wrote a famous essay demonstrating how the style of biblical writers contrasts with what we find in classical literature from the same era. "In the Gospels," wrote Erich Auerbach, "one encounters numerous face-to-face dialogues," and this "direct discourse in living dialogue . . . suffices [to contrast] the writings of the New Testament to classical rhetoric."[2]

In the same era, Amos Wilder likewise noted the prominence of dialogues in the Gospels and claimed that "in each one God, as it were, forces us to give him a face-to-face answer, or, to look him in the eye."[3] In other words, a general quality of encounter hovers over the Gospels as a whole, as Jesus in his role of traveling teacher

---

2   Erich Auerbach, *Mimesis: The Representation of Reality in Western Literature* (Princeton, NJ: Princeton University Press, 1953), 46.

3   Amos Wilder, *Early Christian Rhetoric: The Language of the Gospel* (Cambridge, MA: Harvard University Press, 1964), 48.

encounters many people and groups.

In addition to this general quality of encounter in the Gospels, there is also a specific genre known as the *encounter story*. The two elements that form the foundation of an encounter story are Jesus and a second party in the form of either an individual or group. Either Jesus or the other party can initiate the interaction. For example, Jesus starts the encounter with the woman at the well (John 4:1–42), but in the story of the rich young ruler who asks Jesus what he must do to have eternal life, the young man initiates the encounter (Matt. 19:16–22; Mark 10:17–22; Luke 18:18–25).

The main action or plot in an encounter story is the interaction between Jesus and the other party. In this regard we need to note that dialogue usually carries the story, and encounter stories are thus dramas in miniature. As in a drama, we listen to characters speaking and replying. Usually the best way to lay out the structure of an encounter story is to divide the unfolding dialogue into scenes, and then pay attention to how each of the successive scenes contributes to the ongoing dynamic of the interaction between Jesus and the other party.

Encounter stories have a strong sense of *progression and momentum*. The inciting force consists of either Jesus or the other party initiating verbal contact. Once the encounter has been initiated, we can trace the progress of the dialogue toward its goal, which is usually Jesus' desire to bring a person to belief or correct an error in thinking. Encounter stories are quest stories. Each new statement in the drama advances the process toward the goal of the quest. At the end, the people whom Jesus encounters respond by accepting or rejecting the claim that Jesus has made on them. There is a latent test motif at work, as the people encountered by Jesus either pass or fail a test that is placed before them.

It is a feature of the Gospels that the characters are a representative cross section of humanity. We can place our own heads on the shoulders of the characters in the Gospels. The encounter stories of the Gospels are specimens of the human condition and of how Jesus speaks to that condition. The premise is that *everyone* is encountered by Jesus as the characters in encounter stories are.

Jesus and the Woman at the Well

There are several classic encounter stories in the Gospels, and Jesus' encounter with the woman at the well is one of them (John 4:1–42). In the interest of keeping the story suitably brief for this exercise, the story is printed below in abbreviated form. If you wish to deal with the whole story in your own Bible, here is an outline of it:

> narrative prologue (vv. 1–6)
> scene 1: Jesus' dialogue with the woman (vv. 7–26)
> narrative interlude (vv. 27–30)
> scene 2: Jesus' discourse (not dialogue) to the disciples (vv. 31–38)
> narrative epilogue (vv. 39–42)

The story obviously possesses a classical sense of symmetry. Here is the part of the narrative that comprises the encounter story:

> [7] A woman from Samaria came to draw water. Jesus said to her, "Give me a drink." [8] (For his disciples had gone away into the city to buy food.) [9] The Samaritan woman said to him, "How is it that you, a Jew, ask for a drink from me, a woman of Samaria?" (For Jews have no dealings with Samaritans.) [10] Jesus answered her, "If you knew the gift of God, and who it is that is saying to you, 'Give me a drink,' you would have asked him, and he would have given you living water." [11] The woman said to him, "Sir, you have nothing to draw water with, and the well

is deep. Where do you get that living water? [12] Are you greater than our father Jacob? He gave us the well and drank from it himself, as did his sons and his livestock." [13] Jesus said to her, "Everyone who drinks of this water will be thirsty again, [14] but whoever drinks of the water that I will give him will never be thirsty again. The water that I will give him will become in him a spring of water welling up to eternal life." [15] The woman said to him, "Sir, give me this water, so that I will not be thirsty or have to come here to draw water."

[16] Jesus said to her, "Go, call your husband, and come here." [17] The woman answered him, "I have no husband." Jesus said to her, "You are right in saying, 'I have no husband'; [18] for you have had five husbands, and the one you now have is not your husband. What you have said is true." [19] The woman said to him, "Sir, I perceive that you are a prophet. [20] Our fathers worshiped on this mountain, but you say that in Jerusalem is the place where people ought to worship." [21] Jesus said to her, "Woman, believe me, the hour is coming when neither on this mountain nor in Jerusalem will you worship the Father. [22] You worship what you do not know; we worship what we know, for salvation is from the Jews. [23] But the hour is coming, and is now here, when the true worshipers will worship the Father in spirit and truth, for the Father is seeking such people to worship him. [24] God is spirit, and those who worship him must worship in spirit and truth." [25] The woman said to him, "I know that Messiah is coming (he who is called Christ). When he comes, he will tell us all things." [26] Jesus said to her, "I who speak to you am he." . . .

[28] So the woman left her water jar and went away into

town and said to the people, [29] "Come, see a man who told me all that I ever did. Can this be the Christ?" [30] They went out of the town and were coming to him. . . .

[39] Many Samaritans from that town believed in him because of the woman's testimony, "He told me all that I ever did." [40] So when the Samaritans came to him, they asked him to stay with them, and he stayed there two days. [41] And many more believed because of his word.

The following remarks should be regarded as notes toward an explication of the story and not as a complete analysis:

- Jesus initiates the encounter because he wants to bring the woman to salvation. With this goal always in view, we can trace step by step the progress toward that goal.
- Dialogue is the main element, and the dialogue in turn breaks down into a sequence of interactions in which either Jesus or the woman makes a statement and the other responds or replies.
- Jesus is the one in control of the dialogue, and we can trace his rhetorical or persuasive strategies as he advances toward his desired goal. For example, he in effect poses several riddles to capture the woman's attention and get her thinking in a certain direction.
- The counterpart to tracing Jesus' persuasive strategies is to trace the woman's step-by-step progress in understanding.
- Every story is at some level an example story. In this encounter story, Jesus provides his followers with an example of how to evangelize. But the woman, too, becomes our representative and example, inasmuch as we also need to believe in Jesus as Savior.

Conflict, or Controversy, Story

I will begin by noting a curiosity: while virtually all stories are conflict stories in the sense of being built around one or more plot conflicts, the only body of literature to which the category of conflict, or controversy, story is usually applied is the Gospels. In another surprise, the genre of conflict story *could* be applied to many stories. The situation is (once again) that the category seems natural when we are dealing with the Gospels, while mysteriously receding from view when dealing with other bodies of literature.

In view of the centrality of plot conflict to storytelling generally, it is perhaps no surprise that the largest category of stories in the Gospels is the conflict, or controversy, story. These stories pit Jesus against an opposing person or group. They give the Gospels much of their color and excitement. They contribute to our sense that, despite the episodic plot of the Gospels, the Gospels are built around the situation of conflict. Additionally, the ongoing conflict between Jesus and his opponents keeps moving the individual Gospels to their climax in the trial and death of Jesus.

We can begin our exploration of conflict stories in the Gospels with an awareness that most stories are built around one or more plot conflicts that work their way to a resolution. In stories generally, there is always a protagonist, which in the conflict stories of the Gospels is Jesus. The characters, groups, or social forces arrayed against Jesus are antagonists (and not infrequently villains). Either Jesus or an antagonist might initiate the conflict. Analysis of a conflict story begins by identifying the cast of characters and dividing them into the categories of protagonist and antagonist, the good and the bad.

What I have said thus far might seem to undermine a distinction between a conflict story and virtually every story, but as we keep exploring the subject, differences begin to appear. This will emerge if we get the word "controversy" into the mix, and I will note that the label *controversy story* is a synonym for *conflict story*. The stories we are considering are part of Jesus' career as a controversialist—someone who generated controversy in his society. The conflicts are much more focused on issues and competing viewpoints than most stories are. The primary issue is the claims of Jesus regarding who he is and how people should live. As part of this pattern of controversy, many of the conflict stories narrate how Jesus' enemies tried to trap him, in much the same way that reporters today try to trap a public figure.

There is thus a subtlety that we can analyze in controversy stories. A certain logic is at work, including the logic of entrapment or trickery. Many of these stories are a battle of wits in which Jesus always wins. Often we can trace a back-and-forth rhythm of thrust and counterthrust, offense and defense, attack and rebuttal. A point of similarity between these stories and encounter stories is that both rely heavily on dialogue and drama as the things that carry the story. Conflict stories in the Gospels end in resolution, and we need to analyze what that resolution is. Our final task is to move from story to meaning and determine the lesson that we are to learn from the conflict and its resolution.

With a little streamlining, the following set of questions provides a good analytic framework for the controversy stories in the Gospels:

1. We need to begin with the premise that Jesus is the protagonist and center of attention; who, then, are the antagonists?
2. What is the nature of the hostility of these antagonists?
3. By what means do they pursue their hostility?
4. What back-and-forth rhythm (sometimes a virtual debate) can we trace?
5. How is the conflict resolved, and what lesson can we carry away based on that resolution?

A Controversy over Jesus' Claims

Some of the conflict stories are simple (a brief skirmish in which Jesus quickly silences his enemies), and others are full-fledged stories (such as the controversy that Jesus generates when he heals a blind man as narrated in John 9). The following story falls between these poles:

> Jesus went to the Mount of Olives. Early in the morning he came again to the temple. All the people came to him, and he sat down and taught them. The scribes and the Pharisees brought a woman who had been caught in adultery, and placing her in the midst they said to him, "Teacher, this woman has been caught in the act of adultery. Now in the Law Moses commanded us to stone such women. So what do you say?" This they said to test him, that they might have some charge to bring against him. Jesus bent down and wrote with his finger on the ground. And as they continued to ask him, he stood up and said to them, "Let him who is without sin among you be the first to throw a stone at her." And once more he bent down and wrote on the ground. But when they heard it, they went away one by one, beginning with the older ones, and Jesus was left alone with the woman standing before him. Jesus stood up and said to her, "Woman, where are they? Has no one condemned you?" She said, "No one, Lord." And Jesus said, "Neither do I condemn you; go, and from now on sin no more." (John 8:1–11)

Application of the framework presented earlier yields the following results:

1. Jesus' antagonists are "the scribes and the Pharisees." In the Gospels this is code language for the religious leaders in Jewish society.

2. The nature of their hostility gradually accumulates as each Gospel unfolds, and that becomes a context for sensing what is happening in a given skirmish. The controversial issues were mainly three, and we can catch hints of them in this story: the leaders were fearful of losing their position of dominance in Jewish society; they were angry about Jesus' claims to be divine or to have come from the Father; they opposed many of Jesus' teachings, and in particular they were hostile to Jesus' reinterpretation of traditional beliefs.

3. The Jewish leaders pursue their hostility by establishing a test situation in which they hope they can trap Jesus into denying Old Testament laws and thereby be subject to arrest.

4. The progression of the conflict is as follows: (1) the posing of a conundrum (whether the woman taken in adultery should be stoned, as the Mosaic law prescribed); (2) Jesus' ignoring his opponents by writing in the dust; (3) Jesus' challenging the one who is without sin to cast the first stone; (4) the dispersal of the Jewish leaders in defeat; (5) Jesus' encounter with the woman.

5. Jesus wins the conflict by outwitting the Jews, who cannot meet the requirement of being without sin. The lesson we carry away is the need to extend mercy (seen in Jesus' statement that he does not condemn the woman [v. 11]) and to combine that mercy with a sense of justice that holds people accountable to live righteous lives (seen in Jesus' command to the woman to stop sinning [v. 11]).

LEARNING BY DOING

The "learning by doing" exercise for this chapter gives you a menu of options, using your own Bible for the texts. You should base your decision on how much time you wish to devote to the exercise.

ENCOUNTER STORY

- Along with the story of the woman at the well, the classic encounter story in the Gospels is the story of Zacchaeus (Luke 19:1–10).
- An extended encounter story is the story of Jesus and the two disciples from Emmaus (Luke 24:13–35).

CONFLICT, CONTROVERSY, STORY

- The masterpiece is Jesus' healing of the man born blind (John 9). It has the added attractiveness of being a comic masterpiece, as the Jewish leaders make fools of themselves by trying to deny the obvious. Doing justice to the story will require a large outlay of time.
- A brief conflict story is found in Luke 6:6–11 (Jesus' healing of a man on the Sabbath).

Additional Narrative Forms

This is a good place to remind ourselves of some common descriptors of the Gospels: mixed-genre format, hybrid form, encyclopedic form, and anthology. These labels call attention to the abundance of subtypes that we find in the Gospels, and also the juxtaposition and intermingling of them in a manner that resembles such artistic forms as the mosaic and the collage. The purpose of this chapter is to fill out the narrative genres that have not been covered in the previous chapters.

We need to give an additional meaning to the word "hybrid." This chapter will isolate a series of genres in such a way as to imply that they are "pure" examples of an announced genre. But it is actually hard to find these genres in their pure forms, as I have discovered when assigning students to identify and show the generic features of selected passages from the Gospels. For example, calling stories often include a miracle and could be identified as a miracle story. Conflict stories often include a memorable saying by Jesus and thereby resemble a pronouncement story. Sometimes a witness story is also a recognition story, and it becomes a toss-up as to what to call it. Usually, however, one element is dominant and the other subordinate.

A final preliminary point is that with some of the forms that will be discussed in this chapter, the "generic" narrative considerations of plot conflict moving to resolution and techniques of characterization are somewhat invisible because certain other considerations belonging to the subtypes take precedence. A calling, or vocation, story, for example, is not built around a central plot conflict but simply an encounter and command to follow Jesus.

Miracle Story

Performing miracles is one of the main things that Jesus did during his public years, and the Gospels are accordingly filled with accounts of miracles. These can be plotted on a continuum with expository writing on one end and literary narratives on the other. On the expository end, we find such informational summaries as this: "a great multitude of people . . . came . . . to be healed of their diseases. And those who were troubled with unclean spirits were cured. And all the crowd sought to touch him, for power came out from him and healed them all" (Luke 6:17–19). The discussion that follows will take up fuller narrative accounts that are literary to varying degrees. The typical structure of a miracle story is this:

1. A need is established.
2. Jesus' help is sought.
3. The person in need or acquaintances of that person expresses faith or obedience.
4. Jesus performs a miracle.
5. Characters in the story respond to the miracle and/or to Jesus.

A given miracle story may omit one or more of these elements. Here is a specimen miracle story:

And as they went out of Jericho, a great crowd followed him. And behold, there were two blind men sitting by the roadside, and when they heard that Jesus was passing by, they cried out, "Lord, have mercy on us, Son of David!" The crowd rebuked them, telling them to be silent, but they cried out all the more, "Lord, have mercy on us, Son of David!" And stopping, Jesus called them and said, "What do you want me to do for you?" They said to him, "Lord, let our eyes be opened." And Jesus in pity touched their eyes, and immediately they recovered their sight and followed him. (Matt. 20:29–34)

It is important to describe the exact nature of the miracle (getting the facts straight) and draw a conclusion about what the miracle reveals about Jesus (the interpretive dimension).

Miracle stories in the Gospels are notable for their variety. Some are mere summaries of what happened, while others are full-fledged stories narrated in leisurely fashion. Sometimes the physical miracle is narrated in such a way as to shed the light on Jesus' divine power. But in other miracle stories the focus falls on the recipients of the miracle in such a way as to make them a lesson to us about faith or obedience. Quite often a miracle story merges with another story type, such as a calling story or a pronouncement story.

Pronouncement Story

The pronouncement story is distinctive to the Gospels. It is a brief story in which an event in Jesus' life is paired with a memorable saying or proverb uttered by Jesus. The essential feature of a pronouncement story is that the event and the saying are linked in such a way that we remember them together. Here is a specimen:

> And as he reclined at table in his house, many tax collectors and sinners were reclining with Jesus and his disciples, for there were many who followed him. And the scribes of the Pharisees, when they saw that he was eating with sinners and tax collectors, said to his disciples, "Why does he eat with tax collectors and sinners?" And when Jesus heard it, he said to them, "Those who are well have no need of a physician, but those who are sick. I came not to call the righteous, but sinners." (Mark 2:15–17)

The event and the saying are inextricably linked in our minds, and we remember both of them all the better because of that link.

Despite the seeming simplicity of the form, biblical scholars have subjected it to detailed scrutiny and classification. Sometimes the saying interprets the event that precedes it, casting a retrospective light on the event. Working the other way, an event might lead up to the saying, which is received as the climax of the unit (in contrast to looking backward to the event and shedding light on it). In the example quoted above, the triggering event is not the dinner party but the criticism from the scribes and Pharisees. This criticism sets up the saying, and we give precedence in our thinking to the saying (though this is not to deny that the saying explains why Jesus ate with sinners). The criticism from the Pharisees provides the occasion for the famous saying.

In other instances, we do not feel that the event sets up the saying but the reverse—that the saying helps us understand the event, which is primary. For example, the account of Jesus and his disciples eating grain on the Sabbath (Matt. 12:1–7) eventuates in the saying, "For the Son of Man is lord of the Sabbath" (v. 8). Here the saying interprets the event of eating grain and explains why Jesus did it. We do not assimilate the event in the grain field as leading up to the saying; the important component is what Jesus and his disciples did as they walked through the field.

We should not subject pronouncement stories to excessive analysis. Scholars have multiplied the categories of the pronouncement story in unhelpful ways—stories of correction, objection, commendation, quest, test, and inquiry. The simplicity of pronouncement stories is part of their appeal. At the level of interpretation, what matters most is that the story and the saying belong together. The saying interprets the event, and the event illustrates the saying.

While the pronouncement story is a simple form, it is important to note that *many* events in the Gospels are accompanied by a famous saying of Jesus that we remember as being embedded in the event. For example, in the controversy story known familiarly as "the woman taken in adultery" (John 8:1–11), Jesus utters a statement that lives on in our storehouse of familiar proverbs: "Let him who is without sin among you be the first to throw a stone at her" (v. 7). This story *has affinities with* the genre of pronouncement story, being a hybrid form. Our best procedure is to save the label "pronouncement story" for simple stories where the event and saying are the whole of the story, without additional narrative material. The other stories have a saying intermingled with the event in such a way as to be *like* pronouncement stories.

Calling Story

Another genre that is distinctive to the Bible is the *calling*, or *vocation, story.* I say "distinctive to the Bible" rather than "distinctive to the New Testament" because the Old Testament contains several famous stories in which God called prophets to their life as a prophet. In the Gospels, calling stories are stories in which Jesus calls his disciples or some other individual to follow him as a traveling teacher and miracle worker. After I have explored the genre, I will note that there is a broader sense in which Jesus called multitudes to believe in him (just as there is a general *quality* of encounter in the Gospels in addition to a genre known as encounter stories).

Calling stories are encounters between Jesus and a potential follower in which Jesus extends an invitation or command to follow him. These stories have four ingredients, each of which yields a question that we can ask of the text:

1. The character(s) to whom the invitation is extended: Who is called?
2. The circumstances in which the call occurs: Where does the call of Jesus occur?
3. The nature of the call: To what does Jesus call people?
4. The response to the call: What constitutes the right response to the call of Jesus? Sometimes the answer to that question comes in the form of a negative example of someone who did not choose to follow Jesus, as with the rich young ruler who refused Jesus' invitation to "come follow me" because "he was extremely rich" (Luke 18:22–23).

The characters in the Gospels are at some level representative of people generally. The call that Jesus extends to characters in the Gospels extends to all people in some form.

Here is a specimen calling, or vocation, story from the Gospels:

While walking by the Sea of Galilee, he saw two brothers, Simon (who is called Peter) and Andrew his brother, casting a net into the sea, for they were fishermen. And he said to them, "Follow me, and I will make you fishers of men." Immediately they left their nets and followed him. And going on from there he saw two other brothers, James the son of Zebedee and John his brother, in the boat with Zebedee their father, mending their nets, and he called them. Immediately they left the boat and their father and followed him. (Matt. 4:18–22)

While strictly speaking the Gospel genre of calling story pertains to people whom Jesus invites to become his traveling companions, there is a broader sense in which many stories in the Gospels are calls extended by Jesus to believe in him as Lord and Savior. For example, when Jesus said to the masses, "Come to me, all who labor and are heavy laden, and I will give you rest" (Matt. 11:28), he was calling all people to belief. When Nicodemus visited Jesus by night and was instructed by Jesus about the new birth (John 3:1–21), we assimilate the story as a call for Nicodemus to believe in Jesus. These are not full-fledged vocation stories, but they have *an element of calling* in them.

Recognition Story

In a recognition story, someone comes to a realization of who Jesus is, namely, the Messiah or Savior. Recognition stories are so simplified that they dispense with the element of plot conflict moving to resolution. They simply record the movement of a character from ignorance about who Jesus is to an awareness of his identity. All of the recognition stories in the Gospels end with the ones who come to insight placing their faith in Jesus.

The following list identifies the elements of a recognition story to which we should pay attention as we analyze the story:

- The person who comes to recognition. This person is the protagonist—the one from whose viewpoint we go through the action. It is important to codify what we know about this person.
- The circumstances in which the protagonist comes to a recognition regarding Jesus. What is the setting? Are other people present? How does Jesus fit into this overall scenario?
- The triggering element in this scenario. If there is something that specifically moves the protagonist toward recognition,

what is it? The goal of this question is to reach an understanding of how the protagonist comes to recognition.

- The nature of the recognition. Exactly what does the protagonist come to perceive regarding Jesus?

Here is a specimen recognition story:

Now when Jesus came, he found that Lazarus had already been in the tomb four days. Bethany was near Jerusalem, about two miles off, and many of the Jews had come to Martha and Mary to console them concerning their brother. So when Martha heard that Jesus was coming, she went and met him, but Mary remained seated in the house. Martha said to Jesus, "Lord, if you had been here, my brother would not have died. But even now I know that whatever you ask from God, God will give you." Jesus said to her, "Your brother will rise again." Martha said to him, "I know that he will rise again in the resurrection on the last day." Jesus said to her, "I am the resurrection and the life. Whoever believes in me, though he die, yet shall he live, and everyone who lives and believes in me shall never die. Do you believe this?" She said to him, "Yes, Lord; I believe that you are the Christ, the Son of God, who is coming into the world." (John 11:17–27)

It is easy to apply the list stated above.

To place the genre of recognition story into a broader literary context, the most customary way to structure a literary narrative is to move it toward a moment of epiphany near the end of the story. A moment of epiphany is a moment of revelation and insight. One or more characters in the story experience this moment of epiphany, and so does the reader, who accepts the moment as summing up the main meaning of the story. The reader shares the moment of insight with the character(s) in the story. This is what happens in the recognition stories in the Gospels.

Witness Story

Witness stories are similar to recognition stories. Sometimes both elements are present, producing a hybrid story. In a witness story, someone testifies about who Jesus is or what he has done. There are two categories: sometimes Jesus bears witness to himself, and sometimes another character does so. Here is a specimen:

> The next day he [John the Baptist] saw Jesus coming toward him, and said, "Behold, the Lamb of God, who takes away the sin of the world! This is he of whom I said, 'After me comes a man who ranks before me, because he was before me.' I myself did not know him, but for this purpose I came baptizing with water, that he might be revealed to Israel." And John bore witness: "I saw the Spirit descend from heaven like a dove, and it remained on him. I myself did not know him, but he who sent me to baptize with water said to me, 'He on whom you see the Spirit descend and remain, this is he who baptizes with the Holy Spirit.' And I have seen and have borne witness that this is the Son of God." (John 1:29–34)

The list of questions that we can ask of a witness, or testimony, story is as follows:

1. Who? This is the witness.
2. What? This is the testimony that the witness asserts.
3. Why? This is the proof that the witness sometimes adduces, and it may include the circumstances in which the witness bears testimony or that lies behind the witness's testimony. Sometimes we can draw a link between the circumstances and the specific claims that the witness makes.

When the witness is Jesus himself (as in his seven "I am" discourses in the Gospel of John), the focus is on the content of the claims made about Jesus.

Just as we have seen a general sense of encounter and calling in addition to the specific genres of encounter story and calling story, we should also note broader elements of witness in the Gospels beyond witness stories. For example, the four Gospels themselves are the witness of the writers of the Gospels regarding Jesus. In this sense, the Gospels in total are witness stories. Additionally, there are many moments of witness in the Gospels, interspersed in the stories in which they appear. For example, Matthew 27:27–56 is a crucifixion story, but in the middle of it the centurion is "filled with awe and says, 'Truly this was the Son of God!'" (v. 54). We experience that as a moment of testimony— the moment of epiphany for Matthew's crucifixion story.

Travel Story

The preceding units of this chapter have explored specific narrative subtypes in the Gospels. With the category of travel story, the focus expands from mini-narratives to a meta-narrative for the Gospels as a whole. If we exclude the passion stories that make up a huge concluding segment in all four Gospels, the rest of the material falls loosely into the genre of travel story. It could hardly be otherwise, inasmuch as Jesus lived the life of a traveling teacher and miracle worker during the time covered in the Gospels.

Travel stories have been prominent in the literature of the world at every stage of its history. Their virtues as a story have an enduring appeal to readers. Travel stories provide variety of both adventure and locale. Nothing stands still in a travel story. Along with the variety, we find such standard motifs as danger or difficulty and encounters with friendly and unfriendly people in the places visited. Jesus and his disciples undertake the most elemental of all travels—travel on foot. The stresses of such travel provide an undercurrent of plot conflict. Jesus himself gave us a famous proverb about the rigors of being a traveler: "Foxes have holes, and birds of the air have nests, but the Son of Man has nowhere to lay his head" (Luke 9:58).

Although the genre of travel story does not yield a methodology for analyzing individual units in the Gospels, its explanatory value is nonetheless immense. As with Chaucer's *Canterbury Tales*, the constant journeying is part of the glue that holds everything together (with the governing presence of the central hero Jesus the other part of the glue).

Earlier I suggested that the mosaic and the collage provide good analogies for the collected fragments that make up the Gospels, but those two forms do not quite do justice to what we find as we read the Gospels. The Gospels are fluid, not static. The kaleidoscope of events, dialogues, encounters, and discourses perfectly captures the nature of Jesus' itinerant life. The travel motif provides unity for the Gospels, as virtually everything that we encounter falls under the umbrella "on the road with Jesus." References to journeying, geography, crowds following Jesus, and individuals accosting him along the roadside keep appearing and thereby lend unity to our experience of the Gospels.

The genre of travel story extends to the whole Gospels, not specific units. The situation of traveling is simply something that we are aware of. Occasionally, though, we come upon passages with concentrated references to traveling, and these become something to note as producing a travel story.

LEARNING BY DOING

The following list of narrative units covers all of the genres discussed in this chapter. They do not appear in the order in which they occur in the chapter. Once you have identified the genre of a given passage to your satisfaction, you may wish to review what was said about that genre in the chapter. Then apply that list of considerations to the passage before moving on to the next one. As you work with the material, you will find evidence of the claim made several times in this chapter: the *elements of* a given genre appear in a passage that *overall* falls into another genre. Use your Bible or the Internet to read the passages.

1. Luke 5:1–11
2. John 20:11–18
3. Mark 10:46–52
4. John 4:1–6
5. Mark 6:1–6
6. John 3:25–36

Passion Story

The traditional label "passion story" refers to the concluding segment of the Gospels that narrates the circumstances of Jesus' suffering, crucifixion, death, and resurrection. The word itself is based on the Latin word *pati*, which means "to suffer." All four Gospels move toward the passion of Jesus as their climax. Judged by chapter count, the percentages of the four Gospels devoted to the passion narrative are, respectively, 29, 38, 25, and 38.

Within the individual units, these segments have a distinctive feel that makes them different from the rest of the Gospels. The goal of this chapter is to give readers and teachers confidence in handling the passion narrative. This includes breaking down the final week of Jesus' earthly life into a timeline, and also providing a taxonomy of genres. Anything that makes the passion narrative fall into place will be considered "fair game" for inclusion in this chapter. The goal is to give shape and substance to the long concluding phase of each Gospel.

The positioning of this chapter poses a small difficulty. Since the "passion" segment of the Gospels includes discourses and parables, it would be plausible to place this chapter at the end of the book, after chapters devoted to the discourses and parables. But the passion segment is more thoroughly narrative than discourse, and additionally the passion narrative in its totality, including its discourses, is the climax of the Gospel story and should be included with the narrative sweep of the plot.

The Last Week of Jesus' Life

Literary scholars make a distinction between (1) the chronology of events that make up a story and (2) the plot of a story, which consists of the arrangement of the events for purposes of the story as told. For example, an epic always begins *in medias res* ("in the middle of things") and then takes us back to the start of the chronology of events halfway through the epic. When I teach an epic in my literature courses, I circulate an outline of the events in their chronological order so my students can see the template that lies behind the rearranged sequence that the author chose as the order for the story. This will be helpful for the Gospels as well.

The following list of events during Holy Week aims to be manageable; some timelines are more detailed but less user-friendly. The setting for all events is Jerusalem and the area immediately around it.

SUNDAY
Triumphal entry: a two-mile journey between Bethany (where Jesus stayed each night) and Jerusalem.

MONDAY
Jesus cleanses the temple; religious leaders actively plot to kill Jesus.

TUESDAY
Religious leaders question Jesus' authority; Jesus teaches in the temple precinct and delivers his famous Olivet Discourse.

WEDNESDAY

The Gospels do not assign specific events to this day, which is known in some Christian circles as "silent Wednesday." However, the Gospels do not clearly divide the events of Holy Week into days, so more teaching and conflict with religious authorities might have occurred. Others believe that Jesus remained in Bethany.

THURSDAY

Last Supper (Passover) in the upper room; suffering in Gethsemane.

EARLY FRIDAY

Betrayal and arrest of Jesus in the Garden of Gethsemane; Peter's denial of Jesus; preliminary trials of Jesus.

FRIDAY

Further trials of Jesus, ending in his formal condemnation and handing over to Roman authorities; torture and crucifixion of Jesus; death and burial.

SATURDAY

Jesus' body in the tomb (in some circles called "Holy Saturday").

SUNDAY

Resurrection; appearance to selected women and disciples.

This streamlined chronology provides a skeleton that the Gospel narratives flesh out. The details in the Gospels are mingled together in such kaleidoscopic fashion that it is virtually impossible to keep things straight, thereby capturing the chaotic nature of what happened.

Nonetheless, the time-honored formula of beginning-middle-end allows us to impose an order on the bewildering array of details. In the middle is the crucifixion. With that as the central point of reference, everything before the crucifixion can be seen as a pattern of growing conflict and threat to Jesus, as the events become a relentless death march. Everything that happens after the crucifixion falls into place as aftermath. Seen in this light, the preliminary events point forward to the crucifixion and the events afterward look back to it, allowing us to see that the triumph of Jesus' opponents was only temporary.

Taxonomy of Genres

The passion story is a mini-anthology within the Gospels. Some of the genres that appear are no different formally from earlier parts of the Gospels, though (as noted above) their very position as the lead-up to the crucifixion gives them added voltage and meaning. Other stories carry labels (e.g., trial story and resurrection story) that make them unique within the Gospels. In the following taxonomy, therefore, we should be looking for a blend of the familiar and the new.

Here are the specific genres that make up the passion narratives of the Gospels:

- discourse
- apocalyptic/eschatological discourse
- parable
- straight narrative
- conflict story
- farewell discourse
- prayer
- betrayal story
- arrest narrative

- trial narrative
- denial story
- story of torture
- crucifixion story
- burial story
- resurrection story
- stories of post-resurrection appearance

This is an obviously long list, corresponding to the packed nature of the last week of Jesus' earthly life.

The game plan for the rest of this chapter is to explore the identifying traits of the genres that are somewhat distinctive to the passion story, and to leave the familiar ones untouched because they are discussed in other chapters of this book.

Discourse

Discourses in general will be the subject of a later chapter. The ones that occur in the passion story, however, are not ordinary ones. Because of where they appear in the Gospels, they are connected in our minds with the final week of Jesus' earthly life. Once we are aware of that context, we link these discourses with the last days of Jesus' life.

The passion narrative includes a substantial amount of discourse material in addition to stories. Some of it exists in the familiar form of teaching dialogues, parables, and brief interludes of direct teaching. It is obvious that Jesus did not relent in his teaching ministry during the first half of Holy Week. In addition to the familiar types of discourse intermingled with the narrative units, the passion segment of the Gospels includes several major spoken addresses by Jesus. They fall into three primary genres: apocalyptic/eschatological discourse, the Upper Room Discourse, and farewell discourse.

APOCALYPTIC/ESCHATOLOGICAL DISCOURSE

The eschatological discourses in the passion narrative are "end times" revelations from Jesus. Their ingredients are as follows:

- prediction of future events (both imminent and end-of-history)
- vivid pictures of what will happen at the end of history
- forecasts of great tribulation in a degenerate society
- promise of Christ's return in glory
- prediction of intermediate and eternal divine judgment against sinful humanity
- pictures of eternal reward for believers in Christ upon their entry into heaven

The lead-in to the Olivet Discourse as recorded in Matthew 24:3 hints at all of these: "The disciples came to him privately, saying, 'Tell us, when will these things be [i.e., the destruction of the temple just predicted by Jesus], and what will be the sign of your coming and of the end of the age?'" Jesus' reply is an eschatological discourse that answers both questions.

Upon analysis, the apocalyptic discourses fit naturally into the passion story. The basis for final judgment and redemption is Jesus' triumph over sin and death in his passion and resurrection. The events surrounding Jesus' passion were epoch-making in the same way that the end of history will be. Something new happened with the atoning death and resurrection of Jesus that will reach its climax in the world to come, where all things will be made new.

THE UPPER ROOM DISCOURSE

The Gospel of John contains a major block of material (chapters 13–17) that is customarily labeled the Upper Room Discourse. These chapters record a range of things that happened on the evening before Jesus' crucifixion when Jesus commemorated the Passover with his disciples in an upper room. The material is much more varied than the word "discourse" (singular) implies. For example, two of the seven "I am" discourses of John's Gospel appear in this segment—Jesus as the way, the truth, and the life (14:1–14) and as the true vine (15:1–11). We also find a major discourse on the promised Holy Spirit (14:15–31). Chapter 17 is Jesus' High Priestly Prayer.

FAREWELL DISCOURSE

The farewell discourse is an important biblical genre. It is an address by a leader to his followers when his death is imminent. Examples include Jacob's farewell to his family (Gen. 48–49) and farewell addresses by Moses (Deut. 31–33), Joshua (Josh. 23–24), and Samuel (1 Sam. 12). The motifs that make up a farewell discourse include the following:

- a summoning of followers
- announcement of approaching death
- warning against false teachers
- predictions of woe
- words of comfort and promise
- prayer for those who remain
- appointment of a successor
- instructions regarding how the followers must live after the death of their leader
- worship and prayer

The full-fledged farewell discourse in the Gospels appears in John 13–17. Matthew's Olivet Discourse (Matt. 24–25) contains some of the elements of a farewell discourse, especially instructions about what Jesus' followers can expect in the future.

Stories of Betrayal, Denial, Trial, and Torture

The most distressing stories of the passion narrative are those involving the torture and crucifixion of Jesus, but the sense of heaviness that we experience as we read the passion narrative is not limited to the actual execution and death of Jesus. Events leading up to the crucifixion are equally painful to read. They include the following genres: betrayal story, denial story, trial story, and stories of torture.

Betrayal Story

A betrayal story focuses on a breaking of loyalty by one of two figures in a relationship of trust. Ordinarily this produces catastrophic results for the person who is betrayed. Starting from a position of close relationship and loyalty, the betrayer develops hostility to the other person. The motivation for betrayal is hatred and/or desire for self-aggrandizement, or both. Usually the betrayer achieves his or her goal by divulging something to a third party. Most betrayers end their lives in misery over their act of betrayal.

The story of Judas' betrayal of Jesus is the prototypical betrayal story in the Bible. Judas was motivated by greed for money and probably also disillusionment with the nature of Jesus' messianic plan. The means of betrayal was the worst that we can imagine, namely, a kiss that identified Jesus for the Roman soldiers who came to arrest him.

Denial Story

Denial is a form of betrayal, but a denial story is not identical with the genre described immediately above. Like a betrayal story, a story of denial is built around two people established in a relationship of loyalty. The linchpin of a denial story is that the person who denies the relationship of trust is put in a situation where loyalty is tested. Ordinarily this testing is called a temptation, which implies that there is something in the situation that entices or inclines the betrayer to deny association with the other person. Peter's denial of Jesus is the great denial story of the passion narrative, though the other disciples are equally guilty of abandonment, which is a form of denying loyalty to Jesus. Another shared element in a betrayal story and a denial story is the guilt that the betrayer feels afterward.

Trial Story

The word "arraignment" is a good synonym for "trial" in this context, inasmuch as Jesus' appearance before various officials to be accused and "tried" were more like what we call a "kangaroo court" than a legitimate trial. The passion narrative includes a bewildering sequence (almost a phantasmagoria) of appearances of Jesus before various officials. The sequence began with Jesus' arrest in the Garden of Gethsemane. After that, Jesus was continually under arrest and shuffled from one arraignment to the next. The best way to get a grip on what is happening at a given moment is to codify the action according to the following list:

- the place where the action occurs
- the person or group who is in the position of authority
- the accusers
- the accusations or charges against Jesus
- Jesus' defense of himself
- outcome of the trial or arraignment

Exactly what happened, and in what order, is not easy to decipher in the passion narrative, and this perfectly captures the chaos and secrecy of what transpired on the night before Jesus' crucifixion.

All of the Gospels include a memorable transition and lead-up to the crucifixion that in most Bibles bears a heading to the effect "Jesus is delivered to be crucified." These units can appropriately be included in the category of trial story.

STORY OF TORTURE

Intermingled with the trial stories are brief scenes of torture. The main action in the trial stories is that Jesus was bearing the punishment of the sins of the world. We should assimilate the unfolding action in terms of the suffering endured by Jesus as part of his overall "passion." The scenes of torture highlight Jesus' suffering. Of course the crucifixion was the ultimate torture.

Crucifixion Story

No special tools of analysis are needed to understand the story of Jesus' crucifixion. It is a story that possesses the usual ingredients of plot conflict and sequence, setting, and characterization. The Gospel accounts do not provide a single composite story of the crucifixion. We therefore need to pay close attention to the story as we find it in the Gospel we are reading at the moment.

The first step in analysis is to identify the units that belong to the crucifixion story of the particular Gospel before us. Since the concluding genre in the Gospels is resurrection story (broadly defined to include post-resurrection appearances), it is best to include Jesus' death and burial under the umbrella of crucifixion story. The Gospels give us snapshots of what happened at the crucifixion and burial of Jesus, not a continuous narrative flow. With the units defined, we can apply the following list of questions:

- Starting at an observational or descriptive level, what happens to Jesus in this unit of action?
- Who are the ones who are in control of the crucifixion at any given point, and what can we say about them?
- Who are the onlookers?

- If we include all the people present—the soldiers who performed the crucifixion, the onlookers, and the two victims crucified beside Jesus—how do these divide into two opposed groups (tormentors of Jesus and sympathizers)? What does each group contribute to the crucifixion story?

- The writers of the Gospels are our travel guides through the books that they wrote. They use devices of disclosure that add up to interpretive commentary on the part of the author. Upon close scrutiny, therefore, what interpretation can we see intermingled with the factual account of what happened? What does each Gospel writer highlight for us?

- It is a good reading strategy to imagine yourself present at the events that are narrated. How would you have reacted to what you saw and heard? With just the data of the Gospel accounts at your disposal, how much of the theological meaning of what was happening are you likely to have grasped? For purposes of reading the crucifixion story, it is useful sometimes to make an attempt not to bring into our analysis what we know about the theological significance of what happened on Calvary from prophetic parts of the Bible (including Jesus' "foretelling" statements in the Gospels) and the epistles. Probably we would have understood a great deal less on that day than we do now as part of our familiarity with the prophetic and epistolary parts of the Bible.

The story of Jesus' crucifixion is the saddest story in the world, but it is more than that. A paradox lies at the heart of this story, and fiction writer J. R. R. Tolkien has given us the word "eucatastrophe" to name this paradox. A eucatastrophe is a "good catastrophe." Jesus' crucifixion was the most evil event in history, but it secured the redemption of those who believe in Jesus' substitutionary atonement for their salvation.

Resurrection Story

A resurrection story is one in which a dead person rises from death to life. The resurrection of Jesus is the prototypical resurrection story in the Bible, but it is not the only one. Even in the Gospels we read about "many bodies of the saints" that came out of their tombs in Jerusalem following the resurrection of Jesus (Matt. 27:52–53). The four Gospels tell the composite story of Jesus' resurrection on the third day.

No stories in the Bible have a greater sense of the numinous and awe-inspiring than the stories of Jesus' resurrection. Before we get analytic with these stories, therefore, we need to be receptive to the breathtaking nature of the events that are narrated. Here preeminently we need to imagine ourselves present at the event.

When we turn to analysis, it is important to proceed with the awareness that the resurrection stories have a very important evidential aspect in proving that the Bible is reliable and its supernaturalism worthy of belief. It is therefore doubly and triply important that we pay attention to all of the factual details that the writers have included in their accounts of Jesus' resurrection, with a view toward answering the question of how convincing the data is. Earlier in this guide I covered the genre of witness stories; the resurrection stories are the Gospel writers' witness stories about the resurrection of Jesus. Within the resurrection accounts, too, we find witness stories in the form of the witness of various women and disciples to others in the inner circle about their encounters with the empty tomb, the angel, or Jesus himself.

Other genres covered earlier in this guide are also prominent in the concluding section of the Gospels. The post-resurrection appearances of Jesus combine elements of the recognition story and the encounter story as well as the witness story.

LEARNING BY DOING

Below is a randomly arranged list of passages from the passion narrative of the Gospels. As you work your way through the list, after identifying the genre of a given passage, it will be profitable to look back in this chapter to the description that was offered of that genre, and then apply the methodology provided there to the specimen passage.

1. Matthew 26:14–16; 26:47–50; 27:3–10
2. John 16:16–24
3. Luke 23:26–43
4. Matthew 24:1–14
5. Luke 24:1–12
6. Mark 14:53–65

Discourse and Oration

Up to this point in our journey through the Gospels we can scarcely have avoided being surprised by the complexity we have found. We know that the Gospels are encyclopedic forms that follow a mixed-genre format, but who would have expected that so *many* genres would appear? As we turn now to the discourse material, there will be no lessening of complexity. To get an accurate picture will require our very best thinking.

Defining Terms

What is a discourse, and how does it differ from narrative (the subject discussed up to now in this guide)? A preliminary answer is that narrative deals with action, while discourse deals with thought. A dictionary definition of discourse is "oral or written communication of thoughts." In some contexts, the word "discourse" implies a formal and extended presentation on a subject, but this is not a necessary part of the definition.

As we think about the differing functions of narrative and discourse in the Gospels, we correctly associate discourse with Jesus' teaching, but this is not to deny that Jesus' actions also teach us. Jesus' discourses teach ideas directly, while his actions do so indirectly.

The distinction just stated looks simple, but on the discourse side we actually find a range of ways in which Jesus taught truth. Here are some initial considerations and categories:

- Some of Jesus' discourses consist of addresses on a subject, while some of his teaching occurs in dialogues with people.
- The speeches and addresses range from very brief ones at one end of the continuum to extended ones on the other end.
- Some of Jesus' addresses are expressed in everyday conversational prose, but at the other end of the stylistic continuum we find formal and embellished rhetorical performances that meet classical standards of artistry and rhetorical sophistication. The word "oration" will be used in this guide to denote a formal, polished speech.
- The parables of Jesus fall into the category of discourse material but will receive their own chapter later in this book.
- Under the general rubric of teaching, we can note that some discourses mainly convey information, while others have a stronger persuasive cast as Jesus seeks to *move* his listeners to faith or correct thinking.
- The sayings of Jesus permeate the entire Gospels and are sprinkled throughout the narrative units. The sayings fall into the category of discourse (teaching).

The game plan for the rest of this chapter is to divide the teaching material of the Gospels into three categories: discourses in the form of drama and dialogue; brief discourses or speeches; long and formal speeches called orations.

Dramatic Discourses (or Dialogue–Discourses)

Dialogue is a form of drama, whether the dialogue appears in a written text or is acted on a stage. The process of thinking that goes on in dialogue is usually fluid, following an association of ideas strung together. This is also called stream of consciousness, following the random movement of the mind as it jumps from one idea to the next as the dialogue runs its course.

Before we turn to methods of analysis, we should have actual specimens before us. The following is an example of a brief teaching unit in dialogue format:

> [27] "Do not work for the food that perishes, but for the food that endures to eternal life, which the Son of Man will give to you. For on him God the Father has set his seal." [28] Then they said to him, "What must we do, to be doing the works of God?" [29] Jesus answered them, "This is the work of God, that you believe in him whom he has sent." [30] So they said to him, "Then what sign do you do, that we may see and believe you? What work do you perform? [31] Our fathers ate the manna in the wilderness; as it is written, 'He gave them bread from heaven to eat.'" [32] Jesus then said to them, "Truly, truly, I say to you, it was not Moses who gave you the bread from heaven, but my Father gives you the true bread from heaven. [33] For the bread of God is he who comes down from heaven and gives life to the world." [34] They said to him, "Sir, give us this bread always." (John 6:27–34)

Despite the brevity of the passage, it does not stick with a single idea but instead bounces off an initial idea to something quite remote from the initial idea. Before we notice the evolving nature of the conversation, though, we should note what remains constant, namely, the imagery of food/bread and work.

But the dialogue is not about bread, which is a metaphor for the actual subject. Here is the chain of ideas that unfolds in the passage:

1. the need to engage in work that endures to eternal life (v. 27)
2. the further but related idea that Jesus is the one who gives eternal life (v. 27)
3. the question of what constitutes work for eternal life (v. 28)
4. the need (called a "work") to believe in Jesus (v. 29)
5. the request for a sign to prove that Jesus is worthy of belief, with manna in the wilderness cited as an example of a provable sign from God (vv. 30–31)
6. Jesus' claim to be the true bread from heaven (vv. 32–34)

A seemingly simple dialogue turns out to be complex when considered as a presentation of thought. The most elementary rule for interpreting a discourse of any type (including dialogue) is to ask two questions: (1) What is the topic of the passage? (2) What does the passage say about that topic? For all the meandering of the dialogue between Jesus and his disciples, the main subject is attaining eternal life. The complex of references to food and work and a sign is a vehicle for conveying truth about achieving eternal life. What does the passage say *about* achieving eternal life? That belief in Jesus is the way to attain eternal life. The dialogue is the vehicle for asserting this central idea.

Jesus' dialogue with Nicodemus about being born again represents a longer dramatic discourse:

> [1] Now there was a man of the Pharisees named Nicodemus, a ruler of the Jews. [2] This man came to Jesus by night and said to him, "Rabbi, we know that you are a teacher come from God, for no one can do these signs that you do unless God is with him." [3] Jesus answered him, "Truly, truly, I say to you, unless one is born again he cannot see the kingdom of God." [4] Nicodemus said to him, "How can a man be born when he is old? Can he enter a second time into his mother's womb and be born?" [5] Jesus

answered, "Truly, truly, I say to you, unless one is born of water and the Spirit, he cannot enter the kingdom of God. [6] That which is born of the flesh is flesh, and that which is born of the Spirit is spirit. [7] Do not marvel that I said to you, 'You must be born again.' [8] The wind blows where it wishes, and you hear its sound, but you do not know where it comes from or where it goes. So it is with everyone who is born of the Spirit."

[9] Nicodemus said to him, "How can these things be?" [10] Jesus answered him, "Are you the teacher of Israel and yet you do not understand these things? [11] Truly, truly, I say to you, we speak of what we know, and bear witness to what we have seen, but you do not receive our testimony. [12] If I have told you earthly things and you do not believe, how can you believe if I tell you heavenly things? [13] No one has ascended into heaven except he who descended from heaven, the Son of Man. [14] And as Moses lifted up the serpent in the wilderness, so must the Son of Man be lifted up, [15] that whoever believes in him may have eternal life." (John 3:1–15)

The first paragraph is relatively easy to follow, while the second paragraph seems to introduce irrelevant information into the mix. This is somewhat typical of the element of mystery that lies at the heart of the Gospels. The first paragraph sticks with the topic of the nature of the new birth, which is said to result from the mysterious operation of God's Spirit in the heart of a believer. Verses 9–12 take us to the circumstances of the dialogue and are a scolding of Nicodemus for being "slow on the draw" in his thinking about spiritual reality. The general drift of verses 13–15 is that Jesus will earn eternal life by being "lifted up" on the cross.

Despite the elusiveness of some of the details in a dialogue-discourse, we can always stand back from the particulars and get the general picture. The general thrust of Jesus in this dialogue is that God is the one who achieves and grants salvation in Christ and draws the believing heart to faith.

The general approach for codifying what Jesus teaches in a discourse-dialogue is as follows:

1. Begin with close reading of the text by tracing the contour of topics covered as the dialogue unfolds. Be specific and minute in dividing the dialogue into successive units and labeling them accurately.
2. Having stared at the details, move back from the passage until you can identify a unifying topic for the dialogue as a whole.
3. Having determined what the passage is about, state what it says *about* that subject.

A final bit of clarification is in order. At several points in this guide I have used the label "hybrid forms." Some of the units of dialogue can be viewed as both stories and discourses. For example, the story of Jesus meeting with the woman at the well (John 4:1–42) is an encounter story, but by means of the dialogue Jesus teaches the woman about himself and the proper worship of God. The account is both an encounter story and a dialogue-discourse.

LEARNING BY DOING

I can imagine that many of my readers will initially think that the following passage (Mark 10:35–45) is not a discourse. My reply is that it meets the two essential criteria for the genre that I have been discussing: it is a passage of dialogue, and it teaches us something. It is a dramatic discourse. You can analyze it to test how well you can interpret a dramatic discourse.

> And James and John, the sons of Zebedee, came up to him and said to him, "Teacher, we want you to do for us whatever we ask of you." And he said to them, "What do you want me to do for you?" And they said to him, "Grant us to sit, one at your right hand and one at your left, in your glory." Jesus said to them, "You do not know what you are asking. Are you able to drink the cup that I drink, or to be baptized with the baptism with which I am baptized?" And they said to him, "We are able." And Jesus said to them, "The cup that I drink you will drink, and with the baptism with which I am baptized, you will be baptized, but to sit at my right hand or at my left is not mine to grant, but it is for those for whom it has been prepared." And when the ten heard it, they began to be indignant at James and John. And Jesus called them to him and said to them, "You know that those who are considered rulers of the Gentiles lord it over them, and their great ones exercise authority over them. But it shall not be so among you. But whoever would be great among you must be your servant, and whoever would be first among you must be slave of all. For even the Son of Man came not to be served but to serve, and to give his life as a ransom for many."
>
> Remember the two overriding questions: What is the subject of the passage? What does the passage teach about that subject?

Brief Direct Discourses

Numerically, the dramatic discourses built around a dialogue are in the minority in the Gospels. Most of the discourse material in the Gospels consists of direct addresses by Jesus. We can view these as falling on a continuum. On one end are brief discourses of five or six verses. At the other end of the continuum are longer and more rhetorically embellished discourses called orations, which will receive their own module later in this chapter. Here is a typical brief discourse of the type that we regularly encounter in the Gospels:

> [29] When the crowds were increasing, he began to say, "This generation is an evil generation. It seeks for a sign, but no sign will be given to it except the sign of Jonah. [30] For as Jonah became a sign to the people of Nineveh, so will the Son of Man be to this generation. [31] The queen of the South will rise up at the judgment with the men of this generation and condemn them, for she came from the ends of the earth to hear the wisdom of Solomon, and behold, something greater than Solomon is here. [32] The men of Nineveh will rise up at the judgment with this generation and condemn it, for they repented at the preaching of Jonah, and behold, something greater than Jonah is here." (Luke 11:29–32)

This is a discourse of warning. Its purpose is twofold: to convict the hearers of their sin and to call them to repent. The path by which Jesus pursues these goals is not that of a thesis followed by supporting arguments. Instead, the discourses in the Gospels follow an association of ideas and stream of consciousness. Their sequential unfolding requires a great deal more analysis from us than the essays and discourses with which we are familiar. They resemble what we ordinarily call a meditation on a subject. There is a mysterious and elusive quality to Jesus' discourses that leads us to ponder them instead of quickly grasping them.

The starting point for analysis is to divide the discourse into segments and give each one a label. For the passage quoted above, this yields something like the following:

- Verse 29: Jesus' characterization of his society as being evil and inappropriately (we infer) seeking a sign (left unexplained). We readily assimilate this as a characterization not only of Jesus' day but of the universal human condition.
- Verse 30: Jonah is offered as a sign to Jesus' generation. It is left to us to draw the conclusion that as Jonah called Nineveh to repent, Jesus calls his generation and us to repent. In other words, Jesus is giving his audience an analogy.
- Verse 31: the queen of Sheba is adduced as an example of someone who exerted a major effort to hear the wisdom of Solomon, accompanied by Jesus' claim to be greater than Solomon.
- Verse 32: adducing the repentant people of Nineveh as a standard by which the current generation (in any age) will be condemned for not repenting at the preaching of Jesus.

After identifying the parts (but not without doing so), we can stand back and get the big picture. The subject of this discourse is the need to repent of one's sin. The approach to that subject is to criticize unrepentant people for their indifference to sin and repentance. The means by which Jesus conducts this argument is to adduce "signs" or examples of people from the past who repented. They are offered as models to follow. An argument is ordinarily supported by proof, and we assimilate the people of Nineveh and the queen of Sheba as a form of proof: they saw and heeded the need to repent and will stand in the final judgment because of their repentance.

An obvious lesson that we need to draw from the discourses in the Gospels is that they follow rules that differ from our discourses. They follow some of the rules of literature rather than expository writing, such as giving us images rather than ideas and using a certain indirection that requires our analysis.

LEARNING BY DOING

The following passage will enable you to apply what has been said above about the brief discourses in the Gospels:

> And calling the crowd to him with his disciples, he said to them, "If anyone would come after me, let him deny himself and take up his cross and follow me. For whoever would save his life will lose it, but whoever loses his life for my sake and the gospel's will save it. For what does it profit a man to gain the whole world and forfeit his soul? For what can a man give in return for his soul? For whoever is ashamed of me and of my words in this adulterous and sinful generation, of him will the Son of Man also be ashamed when he comes in the glory of his Father with the holy angels." (Mark 8:34–38)

Here is a checklist of questions to ask:

- What is the subject of the passage?
- How do you know?
- What does the discourse say about that subject?
- By what means does Jesus secure our acceptance of his teaching?

Oration

At the formal end of the discourse continuum we find relatively long addresses. This relative lengthiness seems to produce a degree of formality and rhetorical polish and artistry. The more rhetorical features there are, the more the "how" of the address claims our attention in addition to the "what."

The Gospels of Matthew and John are where we mainly find the orations of Jesus, and the overall design of those two Gospels explains why this is so. The Gospel of Matthew is structured as a back-and-forth movement between units of narrative and units of discourse. There are five blocks of discourse material, and it is only natural that this is where we find the long discourses. Similarly, the Gospel of John is built around seven great "signs" that Jesus performed, and each one is linked to an accompanying discourse that builds upon the sign or explains it. For example, the miraculous feeding of the five thousand (John 6:1–14) leads up to Jesus' discourse on how he is the bread of life (John 6:25–59).

The Sermon on the Mount (Matt. 5–7) is the climax of Jesus' oratorical skill. A complete explication of its rhetorical excellence does not fit the purpose of this guide. As just one example of its rhetorical polish, Jesus uses several groupings of three—instructions on three religious practices (6:1–18), a threefold exhortation to choose right values instead of false ones (6:19–24), instruction on three religious practices (7:1–12), and three great contrasts (7:13–29). The rhetorical technique of repetition is prominent; for example, in chapter 6 the contrasting formulas "you heard that it was said" and "but I say" (or an equivalent) appear six times.

Jesus' discourse on being the true vine illustrates rhetorical expertise on a smaller scale than the Sermon on the Mount:

> [1] "I am the true vine, and my Father is the vinedresser. [2] Every branch in me that does not bear fruit he takes away, and every branch that does bear fruit he prunes, that it may bear more fruit. [3] Already you are clean because of the word that I have spoken to you. [4] Abide in me, and I in you. As the branch cannot bear fruit by itself, unless it abides in the vine, neither can you, unless you abide in me. [5] I am the vine; you are the branches. Whoever abides

in me and I in him, he it is that bears much fruit, for apart from me you can do nothing. [6] If anyone does not abide in me he is thrown away like a branch and withers; and the branches are gathered, thrown into the fire, and burned. [7] If you abide in me, and my words abide in you, ask whatever you wish, and it will be done for you. [8] By this my Father is glorified, that you bear much fruit and so prove to be my disciples. [9] As the Father has loved me, so have I loved you. Abide in my love. [10] If you keep my commandments, you will abide in my love, just as I have kept my Father's commandments and abide in his love. [11] These things I have spoken to you, that my joy may be in you, and that your joy may be full." (John 15:1–11)

The first thing to note is the high degree of unity, in contrast to the dialogue-discourses and brief direct discourses considered earlier in this chapter. Everything in this discourse radiates outward from the central focus on Jesus as the true vine. Literary scholars would speak of a controlling metaphor in the passage. To speak metaphorically itself signals a literary sophistication. Repetition is a major rhetorical device, and this oration illustrates it with repeated words and formulas: vine, bearing fruit, abiding, branch, my Father, and love.

Instead of laboring to delineate the unfolding sequence of topics as we did with discourses considered earlier in this chapter, this oration advertises its structure: the entire passage consists of variations on the central theme of Christ being the vine and believers being branches. All we need to do is name the successive variations on that theme. There is also a central contrast between bearing fruit by abiding in the true vine versus not bearing fruit and being thrown into the fire. Finally, we should note that the discourse does not simply end but is rounded off with a memorable saying (v. 11).

The foregoing analysis shows how our attention just naturally flows in the direction of noticing the "how" of a formal discourse. Is it frivolous to pay attention to the rhetorical beauty and expertise of such a passage? No. Jesus obviously considered it important, as signaled by his composing an address with artistic qualities. The Gospel writers, in turn, considered it important to their enterprise to record the rhetorical nuances of the passage. Furthermore, artistic and rhetorical excellence adds to the impact of an utterance.

LEARNING BY DOING

The following passage (Matt. 25:31–46) is an eschatological discourse about the final judgment. Even though it is a relatively long passage, it is easy to assimilate, whereas the more informal dialogue-discourses and brief discourses often require painstaking analysis before we discern their organization.

"When the Son of Man comes in his glory, and all the angels with him, then he will sit on his glorious throne. Before him will be gathered all the nations, and he will separate people one from another as a shepherd separates the sheep from the goats. And he will place the sheep on his right, but the goats on the left. Then the King will say to those on his right, 'Come, you who are blessed by my Father, inherit the kingdom prepared for you from the foundation of the world. For I was hungry and you gave me food, I was thirsty and you gave me drink, I was a stranger and you welcomed me, I was naked and you clothed me, I was sick and you visited me, I was in prison and you came to me.' Then the righteous will answer him, saying, 'Lord, when did we see you hungry and feed you, or thirsty and give you drink? And when did we see you a stranger and welcome you, or naked and clothe you? And when did we see you sick or in prison and visit you?' And the King will answer them, 'Truly, I say to you, as you did it to one of the least of these my brothers, you did it to me.'

"Then he will say to those on his left, 'Depart from me, you cursed, into the eternal fire prepared for the devil and his angels. For I was hungry and you gave me no food, I was thirsty and you gave me no drink, I was a stranger and you did not welcome me, naked and you did not clothe me, sick and in prison and you did not visit me.' Then they also will answer, saying, 'Lord, when did we see you hungry or thirsty or a stranger or naked or sick or in prison, and did not minister to you?' Then he will answer them, saying, 'Truly, I say to you, as you did not do it to one of the least of these, you did not do it to me.' And these will go away into eternal punishment, but the righteous into eternal life."

Here is a list of questions that will unfold the form and meaning of the passage:

- What is the subject of the passage?
- What contrasts permeate the passage and partly account for its structure?
- What images and metaphors are important?
- What repeated words, phrases, and formulas recur throughout the passage?
- How do the opening and closing verses give the oration an envelope structure? How do they provide an eloquent beginning and close to the discourse?

- How does this oration appeal to our imaginations as well as our minds?

There is much to admire in a beautifully composed oration. We live in a culture that assumes that informal discourse is easy to grasp, while formal discourse is difficult. The orations of Jesus refute that bias: the more artifice there is in Jesus' discourses, the easier they are to follow.

Parable

If we can use the label "fun genre" without irreverence, the parables of Jesus certainly merit that epithet. They are a delight to read, study, and teach. It is no wonder that so many books have been written just on the parables.

The parables epitomize a paradox that is at the heart of the Gospels: *they have a surface simplicity and hidden complexity.* An initial complexity that we can note is that the parables fit the definition of both literary writing and expository writing. They are completely literary in the sense that all their meaning is incarnated in either metaphor or narrative. But the parables also fall into the category of discourse, being designed as vehicles by which Jesus taught truth. The parables were teaching sessions in which Jesus imparted information, as well as storytelling sessions that captivate and entertain us.

The parables of Jesus exist on a continuum from the simple to the complex. On the simple end of the continuum, we find metaphors and similes rather than stories. There are numerous two- or three-verse parables built around the premise that "the kingdom of heaven is like . . ." The only plausible reason to call such a simile a parable is that the narrative parables also use the formula "the kingdom of heaven is like . . ." or something similar. The brief metaphoric parables based on a single analogy require the rules of interpretation that will be given for metaphor and simile in the next chapter of this guide.

As we continue across the continuum, we find stories rather than metaphors or similes—at first very brief ones but eventually ones that can be analyzed with all the tools that we bring to literary narrative (plot, setting, characterization, and so forth). The parable of the prodigal son is an example of a parable that interests us fully at the narrative level. This chapter will cover the narrative parables only. The rules for interpreting the non-narrative ones comprised of a simple metaphor or simile will be covered in the next chapter on poetry.

Folk Tales

The parables of Jesus have been rendered obscure to ordinary Bible readers by their over-interpretation by scholars. We can take a salutary step toward rehabilitating them by placing them into the category of folk literature. Jesus tapped into the folk imagination of ordinary people, drawing upon story qualities that have appealed to the human race from time immemorial.

We can start with the homespun realism of the parables. The world that Jesus portrayed in his parables was the familiar world of his original listeners and of us as well. The actions are universal—planting, harvesting, extending wedding invitations, household routines such as baking bread and traveling to a neighboring town. The people who perform these everyday actions are equally recognizable: farmers, homemakers, fathers and children, migrant workers, widows on a pension, and employees. The literary principle involved here is called verisimilitude, or lifelikeness.

This winsome realism extends to the characters as well. Their most noteworthy aspect is their universality. Only one character

(Lazarus) is named. This anonymity helps make the characters universal types. We have met them before—like characters in the stories of Chaucer and Dickens. While the realism of the parables does not yield tools of analysis per se, it is a quality that partly explains the appeal of the parables, and it is something that can help make the parables come alive in our imaginations. When we teach the parables, giving our students eyes to see the realism will yield dividends.

When we turn to the plot of the parables, certain rules of storytelling as found in folk literature can provide avenues toward analysis. Here is a list of such plot devices:

- the rule of plot conflict (which in folk stories is between obvious good and obvious evil)
- the rule of suspense
- the rule of contrast or foil (e.g., an older and a younger brother with opposite temperaments)
- the rule of simplicity or single action
- as a variation on the last-named trait, the "dramatic rule of two" in which only two characters take part in the action at a given time
- the rule of repetition, especially threefold repetition (e.g., three passersby, three stewards to whom money is entrusted, three types of hostile soil for seed, three categories of abundant harvest)
- the rule of end stress (in which the crucial element comes last, often as a foil to what has preceded, as when the third passerby shows compassion to the wounded traveler after the first two had avoided him)
- the rule of universality (seen especially in universal character types)

These traits can guide us in seeing what is actually present in the text and enable us to conduct a close reading of the text.

One more folk quality that lends universality to the parables is the presence of archetypes. Archetypes are the master images of human experience and literature. Their essential trait is that they recur throughout life and literature. Examples are sowing and reaping, the dangerous journey, lost and found, and the wayward child.

Allegory

Part of the misrepresentation of the parables has been these two longstanding claims (never proved but dutifully passed on in Bible courses): (1) the parables are not allegorical, and (2) the parables embody only one theme or main point. These views have been gradually abandoned during the past four decades, and literary scholars never did accept them. I strongly advise my readers to go with the flow of recent opinion and ignore all claims that the parables are non-allegorical and single-point stories. In this module I will simply show *how* the parables are allegorical, accompanied by the implications of that for interpretation.

The essential principle of allegory is double meaning: a detail in the story stands for something else at a second level. The surface level is the narrative level; the "other" level is what the parable is actually teaching. If we find ourselves in circles (which are few) where it is an insurmountable barrier to claim that the parables are allegories, all we need to do is use the substitute terms "symbol," "symbolism," and "symbolic." The very word from which we get our word "parable" should settle the question immediately. The root word means "to throw alongside." That is exactly what allegory does—it puts a second level of meaning beside the narrative level.

Before exploring this further, we will profit from having an example before us. I have chosen a parable that Jesus himself interpreted, namely, the parable of the sower and the soils. The parable and its interpretation by Jesus are recounted in three Gospels, suggesting that it is prototypical of the parables as a whole. In Mark's account, moreover, Jesus prefaced his interpretation of the allegory with the comment that if the disciples understand this parable correctly, they will "understand all the parables" (4:13). This proves that Jesus' interpretation of this parable was paradigmatic for all the parables. It is highly significant, therefore, that Jesus gave every detail in the parable a corresponding "other" meaning. Here is how Jesus worked out the allegory of this parable:

- the sower = the one who proclaims ("sows") the word (the gospel of salvation)
- the seed that falls long the path = those from whom Satan immediately takes away their interest in spiritual matters
- the seed sown on rocky ground = those who receive the word eagerly but lack root and fall away when tribulation comes
- the seed that falls among the thorns = those for whom the cares of the world and love of riches destroy the impact of the word
- the seed that falls in good soil and produces abundant harvest = those who hear the gospel and respond with belief and godly living

Any story in which a substantial number of narrative details have a corresponding "other" meaning is an allegory, but a story in which *all* the details are allegorical leaves the matter beyond all doubt.

A qualification needs to be stated: starting in the Middle Ages and continuing right to the present day, interpreters have *allegorized* the parables in a way not intended by Jesus. To *allegorize* means to *impose* a secondary level of meanings on a text in a manner not intended by the author. Augustine's allegorizing of the parable of the good Samaritan represents this tradition at its frivolous worst. The traveler to Jericho is Adam. Jericho represents the moon. The thieves are the devil and his angels who stripped Adam of his immortality. The innkeeper is the apostle Paul, and his offer to pay any extra expenses incurred is his counsel of celibacy. Etc.

This is an example of fanciful allegorizing, and it is what gave rise to the false claim that the parables are not allegorical at all. But allegorizing should not be confused with *interpreting an allegorical text*. While there is always a "margin of error" in interpreting the allegory of Jesus' parables, there are safeguards against misinterpretation.

Usually a lead-in by Jesus establishes what the parable is about. For example, many parables begin with the formula that "the kingdom of heaven is like . . ." That sets the process of interpretation in a certain direction, and after that the inner logic of the story makes it clear what details are allegorical (and they need not *all* be allegorical) and what they stand for. The parable of the talents (Matt. 25:14–30) is about what "the kingdom of heaven will be like" (25:1). The context makes it clear that this is an eschatological parable about the end times (being part of the Olivet Discourse). We can safely start with the premise that the parable answers the question, What is required to enter heaven at the end of history? With that as the parameter, the inner logic of the situation allows us to make the following equations:

- the wealthy man who goes on a journey and entrusts his money to his servants = Jesus or God
- the talents (literally weights of money) = all that God entrusts to people (opportunities, gifts, resources)
- the three stewards = representatives of the human race generally, receiving gifts and opportunities in their lifetime
- gaining interest on the entrusted money = serving God well with what he has entrusted

- hiding the money in the ground = squandering the opportunity to be serviceable to God
- the return of the master after a long time = the return of Christ and the final judgment
- the master's commendation of the two faithful servants = entry into heaven
- the master's rebuke of the slothful servant = condemnation in hell

The parables are folk stories, not complex narratives. We need not agonize over them. Furthermore, the folk imagination loves allegory. In folk stories, the allegory is simple and obvious, not an arbitrary puzzle to figure out. If we find ourselves uneasy with our own interpretation of the allegory, a study Bible or reliable commentary will help us toward a mainstream interpretation. The only caution is that the impulse toward allegorizing is ever with us. An example is the view stated in a well-known book on the parables that the talents in the parable represent the Holy Spirit. That bit of allegorizing illustrates a common culprit, namely, giving a detail in the story a narrow or specific meaning rather than a general and obvious meaning.

I also need to sound another caution. The parables exist on an allegorical *continuum* with continuous allegory on the one end, where every detail or nearly every detail in the story has an allegorical meaning. As we move across the continuum, fewer and fewer details have an allegorical meaning. At the very end of this continuum we have what literary scholars call incarnation. This means that the whole story is the meaning. We should not strain to attach allegorical meanings to multiple details if the whole story is the meaning.

A prime example is the story of the good Samaritan. The whole story answers the question that gave rise to the parable, namely, "Who is my neighbor?" (Luke 10:29). This parable is *an example story* more than an allegory: it gives us an example of neighborly behavior. The thing that got Augustine into difficulty with this parable was his assumption that every detail needed to have a second meaning. Can we even call this parable an allegory? My answer is yes because it is so obviously designed to teach a lesson. A heavily didactic ("having the intention to teach") text belongs in a general way to the category of allegory.

How to Interpret and Teach a Parable

The process of interpreting a parable just naturally falls into four phases. Each of these needs to be given as full a treatment as a given parable allows.

The Parable as a Story

We need to begin with straightforward narrative analysis. The primary considerations are plot, setting, and character. If left to our own designs, some of the parables are too brief to yield much only as stories. I will also concede that in the final analysis Jesus' parables require the allegorical level of meaning to reveal their full significance. Another way of stating this is that few of Jesus' parables interest us fully at the narrative level only.

But we should not abandon narrative analysis too quickly. Consulting a few books on the parables will uncover more interesting material on plot, setting, and character than we initially think exists. Experts on the social context of Jesus' life and times can alert us to a wealth of interesting and relevant information about the narrative details. The archetypes in the parables are also a source of interest. The characters are often universal types that come alive despite the scarcity of description. The list of storytelling "rules" listed earlier in this chapter also provides a framework for seeing more narrative voltage than would otherwise enter our experience of a parable. I have consistently found that there is enough narrative technique in the parables to enable me to conduct a relatively full narrative analysis. Let me say again that conducting research into commentary on the parables helps a lot.

INTERPRETING THE ALLEGORY

Having relived the story as a story, we need to ascertain what details are allegorical (i.e., have a corresponding "other" meaning). In most of Jesus' parables at least half of the details have a symbolic "other" meaning. But we need to proceed inductively and allow the inner logic of the parable to guide us in determining the quantity of allegory or symbolism. Having decided what details are allegorical, we need to identify what a given detail represents at the level of the intended allegory (along the lines of analysis outlined earlier in this chapter).

It is important to understand that figuring out the allegory is part of narrative analysis. Because we use religious terminology in stating the allegory (e.g., God, heaven, showing compassion, preaching the word), a certain mindset thinks that the religious meaning of a parable has been explained once we have interpreted the allegorical details. But we *haven't* identified the religious meaning; all we have done is conduct narrative analysis (including identifying the allegory).

INTERPRETING THE THEME(S)

With the story and allegory assembled before us, we need to take the next step of determining what ideas are embodied in the story and allegory. The tried-and-true methodology for determining the themes of any story is to ask what the story is about, and then what it says about those things. A parable might be primarily about one idea, but it is as likely to be about two or three ideas. Even a single metaphor like God as light embodies multiple meanings, not just one.

We can take the parable of the two sons (Matt. 21:28–32) as a test case. The owner of the vineyard is God, as we know from Old Testament symbolism (biblical scholars speak of the traditional symbolic meanings of some of the allegorical details in the parables). The two sons are foils to each other. The first represents an impudence that too quickly sets itself against his father's will. The other son is dutiful on the surface and says what he thinks his father wants to hear. Additionally, this is one of numerous parables built around a principle of reversal and surprise: the seemingly impudent son ends up obeying his father, while the seemingly dutiful son is the one who is disobedient to the father's will. This is the storyline and allegorical thread.

What is the story about? Without the premise that the parables are allegorical, we would interpret this parable as teaching a moral lesson about being an obedient child. But this story is not a moral exemplum; it teaches a spiritual lesson *if* we interpret it as an allegory. This parable is not about being a good family member but about repenting from one's sin. Jesus himself pushes the interpretation in that direction by saying that the story is about "go[ing] into the kingdom of God" (v. 32). What does the story say *about* entering the kingdom? Jesus also gives us commentary on that question. The parable ends (v. 32) by accentuating the need to repent, along with a warning about the judgment that awaits those who do not. The primary theme of this parable is the urgency of repentance.

The parable of the talents (Matt. 25:14–36) provides a second illustration of how to move beyond narrative and allegorical interpretation to a statement of theme. The allegorical identification of the parable of the talents was outlined above. What is the parable about? It is about stewardship, or serving God acceptably. The parable answers the question, What does it take to please God? What the parable says *about* stewardship is multifaceted: God expects and demands productive stewardship; people are called to serve God with the things with which God endows them; final judgment depends on whether or not a person has served God faithfully.

APPLICATION

The final step in mastering a parable is to ask how the themes apply to life. For any text that comes to us from the past, we need to ask two questions: What did it mean then? What does it mean now? Sometimes a parable is so universal that the answer to both questions is the same.

But sometimes the application changes as human history unfolds. Jesus' parable of the workers in the vineyard (Matt. 20:1–16) had a specific application in the first century that has ceased to be relevant today. This is one of several parables that feature a shocking reversal of expectation. Despite the fact that the laborers in the vineyard worked vastly different amounts of time, they all received the same wage (allegorically, redemption and entry into heaven). Is that fair? The theme of the parable is that new standards apply in Christ's spiritual kingdom, which is based on grace rather than merit.

As seen in the book of Acts, in the early decades of the Christian church one of the controversial and bewildering issues was whether Gentile converts needed to practice the burdensome ceremonial laws of Judaism, or whether they were totally free from that burden. Jesus' forward-looking parable teaches that all who work in the vineyard (symbolic of living for God) will be welcomed into glory. Today the application is more general than it was in the early days of Christendom. In any typical Christian group, there is a vast range of seriousness with which people exert themselves for God, as well as differences in the number of years that people serve Christ. Some are even converted on their death-beds. The application of the equal pay for unequal service is that all who believe in Christ receive the same heavenly reward. In the ethic of grace, this is entirely fair, and we should rejoice in that.

LEARNING BY DOING

The greatest of the parables, known familiarly (but not completely accurately) as the parable of the prodigal son, will provide a good opportunity to practice what this chapter has taught. Here is the text:

And he said, "There was a man who had two sons. And the younger of them said to his father, 'Father, give me the share of property that is coming to me.' And he divided his property between them. Not many days later, the younger son gathered all he had and took a journey into a far country, and there he squandered his property in reckless living. And when he had spent everything, a severe famine arose in that country, and he began to be in need. So he went and hired himself out to one of the citizens of that country, who sent him into his fields to feed pigs. And he was longing to be fed with the pods that the pigs ate, and no one gave him anything.

"But when he came to himself, he said, 'How many of my father's hired servants have more than enough bread, but I perish here with hunger! I will arise and go to my father, and I will say to him, "Father, I have sinned against heaven and before you. I am no longer worthy to be called your son. Treat me as one of your hired servants."' And he arose and came to his father. But while he was still a long way off, his father saw him and felt compassion, and ran and embraced him and kissed him. And the son said to him, 'Father, I have sinned against heaven and before you. I am no longer worthy to be called your son.' But the father said to his servants, 'Bring quickly the best robe, and put it on him, and put a ring on his hand, and shoes on his feet. And bring the fattened calf and kill it, and let us eat and celebrate. For this my son was dead, and is alive again; he was lost, and is found.' And they began to celebrate.

"Now his older son was in the field, and as he came and drew near to the house, he heard music and dancing. And he called one of the servants and asked what these things meant. And he said to him, 'Your brother has come, and your father has killed the fattened calf, because he has received him back safe and sound.' But he was angry and refused to go in. His father came out and entreated him, but he answered his father, 'Look, these many years I have served you, and I never disobeyed your command, yet you never gave me a young goat, that I might celebrate with my friends. But when this son of yours came, who has devoured your property with prostitutes, you killed the fattened calf for him!' And he said to him, 'Son, you are always with me, and all that is mine is yours. It was fitting to celebrate and be glad, for this your brother was dead, and is alive; he was lost, and is found.'" (Luke 15:11–32)

By way of reminder, the following is a brief checklist; reviewing parts of the chapter will help fill out the picture if needed:

- Analysis of the story as a story—plot, setting, and characterization. Here is a parable that lends itself to full-scale narrative analysis, so taking a look at chapter 1 of this guide might be a useful review.
- Determining which of the details have an allegorical or symbolic "other" meaning, and additionally identifying what each of these represents at the allegorical level.

- Formulating an understanding of what the parable is about (it is about multiple topics), and further what it says *about* those topics. These are the themes of the parable.
- How do these themes apply to people (including oneself)?

Poetry and Proverb

With poetry and proverb we move into the domain known as style. Style is an important aspect of the Gospels. Whether or not we take time to analyze that style, we are continuously in touch with it as we read. In all communication, there is no content without the form in which that content is expressed and embodied. Style is an aspect of form. Additionally, the impact the Gospels have on us is due partly to stylistic effects. For example, the very style of Luke's nativity story (2:1–20) is part of the sway that the story holds over us.

The two topics covered in this chapter (poetry and proverb) encompass both genre and style. On the one hand, we can speak of poetry and proverb as genres. But when we turn those nouns into adjectives—poetic and aphoristic—we are speaking of a general stylistic tendency of the Gospels that can appear in any of the genres.

Distinguishing between Poetry and Poems

We need to begin by decisively distinguishing between poetry and poems. Poetry is a form of spoken or written discourse. Poets speak a "language" all their own, known as the poetic idiom. It is "the language poets use" (as a book title states it). This language can appear in isolated form in any kind of discourse, including prose. Examples of poetic language are imagery, metaphor, and other figures of speech. Wherever they appear, they need to be analyzed in keeping with their poetic nature. When Jesus says in a prose discourse that his followers are the salt of the earth (Matt. 5:13), the metaphor of salt falls into the category of poetry.

Poetry thus refers to a type of thinking, imagining, and oral or written expression. The term "poem" refers to a whole composition made out of poetry. Additionally, a poem falls into one or another verse form, which becomes an additional identifying trait.

If we apply the two categories of poetry and poems to the Gospels, we can say first that the Gospels are continuously poetic, chiefly in the oral statements of Jesus. Jesus is one of the world's most famous poets because his sayings, conversations, parables, and discourses are filled with imagery and figures of speech. The number of poems in the Gospels is relatively small, though there is a category known as poetic prose (also called prose poems) that slightly expands the corpus of poems in the Gospels.

Poetry

The logical starting point is to explore the *poetry* (as distinct from *poems*) of the Gospels—the presence of imagery and figures of speech in all of the Gospel genres. To get a handle on the subject, I will provide a taxonomy of the most important poetic devices found in the Gospels, accompanied by definitions, illustrations from the Gospels, and rules of analysis.

IMAGE AND IMAGERY

"Image" is a word naming a concrete action or thing. Light, water, and taking up a cross and following Jesus are images. "Imagery" is the word used to name the total accumulation of images in a poem or passage, or a pattern of related images in such a passage.

Thus nature imagery figures prominently in Jesus' discourse against anxiety in Matthew 6:25–34.

The "straight image" (as opposed to a metaphor or simile) does not state a comparison; it stands by itself. Such an image requires three levels of analysis or interpretation:

1. We need to make sure that we have pictured the literal, physical image accurately. Usually our own experience of that image will give us all the information that we need, but it is important to ponder on the image to drink in all of its facets. Sometimes we need help from biblical scholarship (via a study Bible or reliable Internet site or Bible commentary) to grasp the image. For example, Jesus' parable of the ten virgins (Matt. 25:1–13) turns upon lamps and oil. These lamps were small, handheld lamps with very small capacity for the oil that provided the light. They required a flask with a reserve supply of oil to assure the carrier of fuel when light was needed.

2. Often we need to reflect on the connotations of an image. Connotations are associations and meanings that surround an image beyond the denotative dictionary definition. For example, Jesus used the image of a house built upon a rock to picture the choice to obey his words (Matt. 7:24). The literal picture is a house built on a firm foundation. The connotations of that image are careful planning on the part of the builder, stability, and endurance in storms. Connotations potentially include emotional meanings, such as a feeling of safety when we picture a house upon a rock that stands unharmed by a storm.

3. In addition to denotation and connotation, we need to explore the logic of an image in its context. The right question to ask is, Why did Jesus choose this particular image for the subject under consideration? For example,

what is the logic of Jesus telling us to "consider the lilies of the field" (Matt. 6:26) in a discourse against anxiety?

METAPHOR, SIMILE, AND SYMBOL

A metaphor is an implied comparison between two things that does not use the formula "like" or "as"; for example, "I am the bread of life" (John 6:35). A simile uses "like" or "as" but is otherwise just like a metaphor: for people who do not remain watchful, the final day will "come upon [them] suddenly like a trap" (Luke 21:34). The essential principle of both metaphor and simile is analogy or correspondence, as one thing is compared to another to illuminate it. The rules for interpreting metaphor and simile are the same, as follows:

- Metaphors and similes begin as an image and then become a comparison. We can refer to the two halves of the comparison as level A and level B. At level A, we need to apply exactly the same analysis as prescribed above for the straight image—the literal, physical properties of the phenomenon, its connotations, and the logic of its appearing in this particular context.

- The word "metaphor" is based on two Greek words (*meta* and *pherein*) meaning "to carry over." That is the essential transaction: having fully experienced the image at level A, we need to carry over those meanings to level B, which is the actual subject of the statement. Jesus' metaphor that he is the good shepherd (John 10:14) offers an illustration. What does a good shepherd do? In the physical sphere, he provides physical provision to sustain the lives of his sheep, and he protects his sheep from harm. The metaphor has transacted its intended business when we *carry over* those meanings from a shepherd to Jesus, and physical provision and safety to spiritual provision and safety.

Symbol

Symbol is usually allotted a separate niche in lists of figures of speech, but for the Gospels it is difficult to differentiate it from metaphor and simile. Is Jesus as light of the world a metaphor or symbol? It can accurately be called both. I will simply define symbol, therefore, and leave it to my readers to decide whether or not to use it interchangeably with metaphor.

A symbol exists at a literal level, but this literal image represents or stands for one or more other things. This other set of meanings is the more important aspect of a symbol in the sense that the symbolic meanings are what the statement is really about. Jesus' statement that "a city set on a hill cannot be hidden" (Matt. 5:14) is not *about* the physical location of a literal city, although the impact of the statement depends on our imagining a city on a hill. The passage is about believers living godly lives that testify to God. The city on a hill is a symbol.

Before leaving the subject of metaphor, simile, and symbol, we need to note a complexity. The parables of Jesus function as comparisons in the same way that metaphors and similes do. In fact, the brief ones *are* simply metaphors or similes. Even the full-fledged narrative parables function in such a way that what has been said above about metaphor, simile, and symbol can be applied to parables. Perhaps the best way to view this is to say that the full-fledged parables *have affinities or correspondence to* metaphor, simile, and symbol.

Hyperbole

Hyperbole is exaggeration for the sake of effect. A hyperbolic statement is never literally true, but by means of its exaggeration it gets us to see the truth even more vividly than we would with a literal statement. In this, it obeys a general rule of poetry to defamiliarize something that has become so routine that we do not give it the attention it deserves. Poetry is partly an attempt to overcome the cliché effect of familiar language or ideas that have become threadbare or lifeless.

Jesus did not share a common skittishness about hyperbole. It was one of his favorite figures of speech or rhetorical devices. He spoke of a camel going through the eye of a needle (Matt. 19:24), a mustard plant that becomes a huge tree in which birds build nests (Luke 13:19), leaving the dead to bury their own dead (Matt. 8:22), and hating the members of our own family (Luke 14:26). Jesus seems to have particularly enjoyed the gigantesque statement as a rhetorical device.

When do we ourselves use hyperbole? We use it to express strong feeling, to state extreme conviction about something, and to get people to take notice of a statement. The same uses can be assumed to be present in Jesus' hyperbolic statements. How should we interpret a hyperbole? The first thing is to recognize it and call it what it is—a conscious exaggeration used for the sake of effect. Then we need to analyze what truth is expressed by the exaggeration. Jesus' statement that we must hate our father and mother means, once we have scaled back the element of exaggeration, that we must value God more than our earthly family and *potentially* we must choose God over family.

Paradox

A paradox is a seeming contradiction that upon analysis can be seen to express truth. Jesus was as fond of paradox as he was of hyperbole. In Jesus' paradoxical imagination, the first will be last and the last first (Matt 20:16), the person who finds his life will lose it and the one who loses his life will find it (Matt. 10:39), and the one who would be first must be slave of all (Mark 10:44). Like hyperbole, a paradox jolts us out of complacent thinking and shocks us into confronting a truth.

A paradox requires two interpretive actions from us. The first is to identify a paradox when we find it. At the surface level it is a contradiction, and we need to let the contradiction register with us. But a paradox is an *apparent* contradiction, not a genuine one. If we analyze it properly and *resolve* the contradiction, we can see that it expresses truth. For example, people who are last in worldly standing, either literally or by self-renunciation, can be first by trusting in God and thereby gaining eternal life. A paradox functions like a riddle, initially baffling us and then teasing us into resolving the apparent contradiction.

Poems

Poems are compositions made out of poetry (defined above as a way of thinking, imagining, speaking, and writing). As compositions, poems are unified by a single theme. The individual parts can be formulated as variations on that theme. Poems are more concentrated than ordinary discourse and require closer analysis than ordinary discourse does. They have line-by-line deliciousness.

A poem is also embodied in a verse form. In the Bible, this verse form is parallelism. Biblical poetry does not have rhyming lines but features parallelism of thought. Our eye immediately sees this as we look at a biblical poem. In parallelism, at least part of the first line is repeated or balanced by all or part of the second line. The grammatical form is retained in both lines (or more than two lines). Here is an example of parallelism (Matt. 7:2):

> For with the judgment you pronounce you will be judged,
> and with the measure you use it will be measured to you.

Verse form increases the impact of a statement and is an artistic element that we can enjoy as an example of verbal beauty.

The rules for reading and explicating a poem are as follows. The basic organization is a three-part structure: a beginning, a middle, and an end. The beginning establishes the subject of the poem; the middle develops it with a series of separate variations on that theme; and the conclusion rounds the poem out with a note of finality. That constitutes the skeleton of the poem. The meaning resides in the poetic texture—the individual images and figures of speech. The poetic texture is what chiefly occupies us when analyzing or teaching a poem.

How many poems are there in the Gospels? Relatively few. The following is a beginning list:

- John 1:1–18 is a Christ hymn; it appears in our Bible as prose but is so patterned that it can be easily cast into the form of poem with parallelism.
- Four nativity poems: Mary's Magnificat (Luke 1:46–55), Zechariah's song (Luke 1:67–79), the angels' song (Luke 2:14), and Simeon's song (Luke 2:29–32).
- Three passages in Jesus' Sermon on the Mount: the beatitudes (Matt. 5:1–12), the Lord's Prayer (Matt. 6:9–13), and the discourse against anxiety (Matt. 6:25–34), which can easily be printed as a poem.

Additionally, the Gospels include many brief quotations from the Old Testament, and simply paging through the Gospels will show at once that many of these are excerpts from poems, as their offset positioning in the prevailing prose of the Gospels shows (e.g., Luke 4:8, 10, 11, 18–19).

But this does not exhaust the subject. Some of Jesus' orations are so patterned and so replete with parallel phrases and clauses that they *could* be printed as poems. Here is an example (Matt. 7:7–8):

Ask, and it will be given to you;
seek, and you will find;
knock, and it will be opened to you.

For everyone who asks receives,
  and he who seeks finds,
    and to the one who knocks it will be opened.

The passage lacks the formal opening and closing of a complete poem, but in every other way it is a short poem, even though it appears as prose in our Bibles.

LEARNING BY DOING

There are relatively few poems in the Gospels; most of the poetry is scattered throughout the prose narratives and discourses, and that is where the application of the foregoing discussion primarily occurs. I have therefore gathered some prose passages that require analysis of the imagery and figures of speech. Your task is to identify and interpret the figures of speech. Remember that the image counts as a figure of speech.

- "Enter by the narrow gate. For the gate is wide and the way is easy that leads to destruction, and those who enter by it are many. For the gate is narrow and the way is hard that leads to life, and those who find it are few. Beware of false prophets, who come to you in sheep's clothing but inwardly are ravenous wolves. You will recognize them by their fruits" (Matt. 7:13–16).

- And he said to all, "If anyone would come after me, let him deny himself and take up his cross daily and follow me. For whoever would save his life will lose it, but whoever loses his life for my sake will save it. For what does it profit a man if he gains the whole world and loses or forfeits himself?" (Luke 9:23–25).

- He said therefore, "What is the kingdom of God like? And to what shall I compare it? It is like a grain of mustard seed that a man took and sowed in his garden, and it grew and became a tree, and the birds of the air made nests in its branches." And again he said, "To what shall I compare the kingdom of God? It is like leaven that a woman took and hid in three measures of flour, until it was all leavened" (Luke 13:18–21).

- "I am the true vine, and my Father is the vinedresser. Every branch in me that does not bear fruit he takes away, and every branch that does bear fruit he prunes, that it may bear more fruit. Already you are clean because of the word that I have spoken to you. Abide in me, and I in you. As the branch cannot bear fruit by itself, unless it abides in the vine, neither can you, unless you abide in me. I am the vine; you are the branches. Whoever abides in me and I in him, he it is that bears much fruit, for apart from me you can do nothing. If anyone does not abide in me he is thrown away like a branch and withers; and the branches are gathered, thrown into the fire, and burned" (John 15:1–6).

Proverb or Saying

It is highly unlikely that the Gospels began as collections of Jesus' sayings, but the very fact that this theory gained currency in earlier eras of New Testament scholarship hints at the importance of Jesus' sayings. These sayings are proverbs or aphorisms ("famous quotations"). There are two dimensions of a proverb that this module will explore: (1) the traits of a proverb that we can recognize and admire as an example of verbal beauty and craftsmanship; (2) rules for interpreting and applying a proverb.

The traits of a proverb, accompanied by illustrations, are as follows:

- A proverb is apt and memorable. Even on a first hearing or reading, the effect is striking, and we know that it is worthy of memory. Example: "Where your treasure is, there will your heart be also" (Luke 12:34).
- A proverb is simultaneously simple and profound and even complex. On the simplicity side, a proverb is short and easily grasped. But often a proverb requires us to figure it out, and additionally we never get to the end of its application. Example: "Remember Lot's wife" (Luke 17:32).
- A proverb expresses a high point of insight; it captures an idea at its clearest focus, much as a camera brings a scene into its focus. Often a proverb in the Gospels comes at the end of a narrative or discourse unit, and we come to expect its appearance as the culminating insight of the passage. Example: "For the Son of Man came to seek and to save the lost" (Luke 19:10).
- Part of the punch of a proverb resides in its use of special resources of syntax (sentence structure), starting with a more-than-ordinary succinctness but often including such rhetorical devices as contrast and parallelism. Many proverbs in the Gospels use contrast, repetition, and balance of sentence elements. Examples: "Seek, and you will find; knock and it will be opened to you" (Luke 11:9). "Everyone who exalts himself will be humbled, but the one who humbles himself will be exalted" (Luke 18:14).
- Proverbs sometimes use poetic or figurative language. Examples: "You are the light of the world" (Matt. 5:14). "The harvest is plentiful but the laborers are few" (Matt. 9:37; Jesus is not talking about a grain harvest but a metaphoric spiritual one).

What interpretive activities do proverbs require of us? One response is simply to admire and marvel at them. There is an aesthetic aspect to how we assimilate a proverb, as we celebrate it as an example of verbal beauty. Additionally, it often yields insight to ask and answer the question, What is there about this proverb that strikes me or that accounts for its power? The list of traits offered above helps to answer that question. A great aphorism does not put an end to reflection on a subject but is the starting point for reflection. Memorizing the sayings of Jesus is a useful thing to do, and I will note that with a proverb, getting the wording precisely correct is key to its impact (a paraphrase or approximation does not suffice).

An aphorism is not intended only to lead us to marvel at its beauty and reflect on its meaning but to apply it to our lives. The place where a proverb or saying lives most fully is the everyday circumstance of life where it applies.

LEARNING BY DOING

Below is a collection of proverbs that will enable you to practice what the foregoing module has imparted:

- "Come to me, all who labor and are heavy laden, and I will give you rest" (Matt. 11:28).
- "Whoever follows me will not walk in darkness, but will have the light of life" (John 8:12).
- "What does it profit a man to gain the whole world, and forfeit his life?" (Mark 8:36).
- "Each tree is known by its own fruit" (Luke 6:44).
- "Render to Caesar the things that are Caesar's, and to God the things that are God's" (Mark 12:17).

A Gospel Miscellany

The Gospels are so encyclopedic that despite the abundance of literary genres and forms already discussed in this guide, a number of important ones remain. I have brought them together for brief treatment under a designation that was dear to literary people in the Renaissance and is still current. A dictionary defines a miscellany as "a collection of different items; a mixture; an assortment of different pieces of writing." This chapter will discuss forms of writing in the Gospels that are too important not to place before my readers before I conclude this guide.

Varieties of Prose Style

Prose style is a standard consideration in high school and college literature courses, as well as a subject of discussion by literary critics. The premise underlying this interest is that prose style is a form of art and verbal craftsmanship that can be enjoyed for its beauty. Additionally, analysis of prose style sometimes enables us to explain the impact of a passage on us.

Prose style exists on a continuum, with plain and unadorned style on one end and embellished and grand style on the other. The narrative sections of the Gospels are the very touchstone of simple prose. There is no more beautiful example than Luke's story of the birth of Jesus, as seen in the following excerpt:

> And Joseph also went up from Galilee, from the town of Nazareth, to Judea, to the city of David, which is called Bethlehem, because he was of the house and lineage of David, to be registered with Mary, his betrothed, who was with child. And while they were there, the time came for her to give birth. And she gave birth to her firstborn son and wrapped him in swaddling cloths and laid him in a manger, because there was no place for them in the inn. (Luke 2:4–7)

This is more dignified than the idiom of the dormitory or coffee shop, but it is nonetheless simple and unadorned. There is a simplicity that diminishes and a simplicity that enlarges. The simple dignity of the prose style of the Gospels exalts us.

But the high style also receives a place in the Gospels, chiefly in the oratory of Jesus and in the poems scattered throughout the Gospels (including quotations from the Old Testament). The balanced repetition of phrases and the long sentence construction in the following passage, as well as the presence of rhetorical questions, place the passage in the best tradition of embellished prose:

> Therefore I tell you, do not be anxious about your life, what you will eat or what you will drink, nor about your body, what you will put on. Is not life more than food, and the body more than clothing? Look at the birds of the air: they neither sow nor reap nor gather into barns, and yet your heavenly Father feeds them. Are you not of more value than they? . . . Consider the lilies of the field, how they grow; they neither toil nor spin, yet I tell you, even Solomon in all his glory was not arrayed like one of these. (Matt. 6:25–26, 28–29)

All levels of prose in the Gospels are uniquely powerful and beautiful. We can admire them as examples of verbal beauty.

Satire

Satire is a very important genre and presence in the Gospels, and we will read and teach the Gospels better if we are aware of this. Satire is an attack on (or exposure of) vice or folly. A piece of satire has four elements, and each of these needs to be analyzed when we read or teach a piece of satire. They are as follows:

- one or more objects of attack
- a satiric vehicle (such as narrative, metaphor, direct denunciation) that embodies the attack
- a satiric norm (the standard of truth or correctness by which the criticism is being conducted)
- a dominant satiric tone, of which there are only two possibilities—harsh and biting or light and even humorous

These are the terms of engagement for mastering any satiric passage.

There is an additional framework that we need to have in mind. The world's satire falls into two main categories, or traditions. In the plainspoken tradition, the satirist adopts a fiery pose and directly denounces vice, error, or folly. Common features used by the plainspoken satirist are these:

- the satirist's projection of himself as a person of undistinguished social standing (as Amos the shepherd does in the Old Testament)
- loose and even rambling structure, jumping from one detail to the next
- simple or common prose style, approximating the ordinary speaking voice

- vituperation and invective (bitter and insulting language)
- direct denunciation of vice and people
- attack on groups rather than individuals
- sense of urgent involvement
- bitter rather than light tone

Jesus' denunciation of the Pharisees in Matthew 23:1–36 illustrates this type of satire to perfection. Here is an excerpt (vv. 25–28):

Woe to you, scribes and Pharisees, hypocrites! For you clean the outside of the cup and the plate, but inside they are full of greed and self-indulgence. You blind Pharisee! First clean the inside of the cup and the plate, that the outside also may be clean.

Woe to you, scribes and Pharisees, hypocrites! For you are like whitewashed tombs, which outwardly appear beautiful but within are full of dead people's bones and all uncleanness. So you also outwardly appear righteous to others, but within you are full of hypocrisy and lawlessness.

The other tradition of satire is the sophisticated tradition. The satirist is not an angry person who might be pictured as leading a protest march but a sophisticated literary craftsman, submerged in a carefully composed story. The author is not only the denouncer of vice but also a literary composer. Jesus' parable of the enterprising farmer illustrates this tradition:

[13] Someone in the crowd said to him, "Teacher, tell my brother to divide the inheritance with me." [14] But he said to him, "Man, who made me a judge or arbitrator over you?" [15] And he said to them, "Take care, and be on your guard against all covetousness, for one's life does not consist

in the abundance of his possessions." [16] And he told them a parable, saying, "The land of a rich man produced plentifully, [17] and he thought to himself, 'What shall I do, for I have nowhere to store my crops?' [18] And he said, 'I will do this: I will tear down my barns and build larger ones, and there I will store all my grain and my goods. [19] And I will say to my soul, Soul, you have ample goods laid up for many years; relax, eat, drink, be merry.' [20] But God said to him, 'Fool! This night your soul is required of you, and the things you have prepared, whose will they be?' [21] So is the one who lays up treasure for himself and is not rich toward God." (Luke 12:13–21)

If we apply the list of satiric considerations to this parable, we find the following:

- Object of attack: worldly mindedness and devotion to riches. Wealth is not held up to rebuke but the state of mind and soul that it engenders, as seen in the farmer's overheard speech in verse 19. The surrounding aphorisms also help us to label the object of attack: verse 14 speaks of covetousness, and verse 21 of laying up treasure for oneself. This seemingly simple parable is already showing amazing complexity, in the tradition of sophisticated satire.
- Satiric vehicle: narrative. Jesus the satirist is completely submerged in this skillfully composed story. The protagonist is the enterprising farmer. His chief traits are his preoccupation with earthly success and moneymaking, his spiritual complacency (as seen in his address to his soul in v. 19), and his misplaced trust in earthly security (v. 19). The brief plot does not turn on plot conflict but rather a surprise ending in which the farmer dies immediately after contemplating his building project.

- Satiric norm (the standard by which the behavior that is held up to rebuke is judged): multiple. It is unusual for a satire to be as multiple as this one. What principles did the farmer violate? The surrounding aphorisms suggest two preliminary answers: the farmer ignored the command not to be covetous of (excessively devoted to) worldly possessions (v. 15), and he was not rich toward God (v. 21). Additionally, the farmer's presumption that he would live many years (v. 19) shows his disregard for the fleetingness of life (the surprise ending). In regard to the latter, one satiric norm is living in an awareness of human mutability; the farmer did not live in that awareness.
- Satiric tone: light. The farmer is an example of ridiculous folly. He is a fool (v. 20) in the tradition of literary and real-life dunces. Despite the seriousness of the issues raised in this parable, Jesus' strategy is to give us an example of laughable folly. Even the farmer's building strategy of tearing down his barns instead of simply adding to his farmstead makes no sense.

Riddle

I have long claimed that the Gospels possess a mysterious and riddling quality. Then Tom Thatcher published a whole book on the subject titled *Jesus the Riddler: The Power of Ambiguity in the Gospels*.[4] Here are some of the categories that fit under the rubric of riddle:

- the allegory of Jesus' parables, requiring a reader or listener to figure out the correspondences

---

4   Tom Thatcher, *Jesus the Riddler: The Power of Ambiguity in the Gospels* (Louisville: John Knox Press, 2006).

- in addition to the allegory of all the parables, the problematical storyline of some of them (such as the parable that praises a dishonest manager [Luke 16:1–9])
- mysterious statements by Jesus that left his original listeners baffled (the Gospel of John records nine instances of misunderstood statements made by Jesus)
- some of Jesus' metaphors that leave us wondering what they mean (e.g., regarding the person who believes in him Jesus said, "Out of his heart will flow rivers of living water" [John 7:38])
- scattered incidents where Jesus told someone not to disclose a miracle that he had performed, leading us to wonder why
- the paradoxes of Jesus (such as "the first shall be last and the last first"), which initially perplex us and then prompt us to resolve the apparent contradiction in a manner akin to solving a riddle
- sayings or aphorisms that leave us wondering what they mean (as when Jesus ends his rebuttal of the Pharisees with the mysterious saying, "Yet wisdom is justified by all her children" [Luke 7:35])

Two formulas that Jesus sometimes used may have been a conventional way of signaling that he was posing a riddle, namely, "He who has ears to hear, let him hear," and, "What do you think?"

Any statement that does not make immediate sense is akin to a riddle. Many of Jesus' statements in the Gospels fall into that category. Jesus said that "everyone will be salted with fire" (Mark 9:49), and in the next verse he commanded, "Have salt in yourselves"; what does that mean? "Remember Lot's wife" (Luke 17:32); *what* are we expected to remember about her? These are riddles of a sort.

Humor

With riddle and humor, we are partly speaking of a general quality found in the Gospels, not a genre per se. I would prefer to speak of "the rhetoric of the riddle" and "the rhetoric of humor" in the discourses and sayings of Jesus. Still, we should not be intimidated by the thought that Jesus enjoyed humor and incorporated it into his conversations and speeches.

Multiple books have been written on the humor of Jesus, but the classic is Elton Trueblood's *The Humor of Christ.*[5] I do not have space to explore this subject in detail, so I will simply list some of the categories of humor that we find in the Gospels:

- Situation comedy in some of the events recorded in the Gospels, as in the story of the healing of the blind man in John 9.
- The preposterous or gigantesque: swallowing a camel (Matt. 23:24); a person's right hand not knowing what the left hand is doing (Matt. 6:3).
- Sarcasm, as when Jesus, facing a crowd ready to stone him, said, "I have shown you many good works from the Father; for which of them are you going to stone me?" (John 10:32).
- Touches of humor in Jesus' observations about life, as when he finished a discourse against anxiety with the comment, "Sufficient for the day is its own trouble" (Matt. 6:34).
- Humorous rhetorical questions: "Are grapes gathered from thornbushes, or figs from thistles?" (Matt. 7:16).
- Word play. The Greek words "Peter" and "rock" sound similar, so Jesus pinned the nickname "the rock" ("Rocky," in our parlance) on Peter. There is also humorous irony in this name: Peter was an unstable and unpredictable personality, and the idea of his being a rock is akin to calling

---

5   Elton Trueblood, *The Humor of Christ* (New York: Harper & Row, 1964).

a habitually late person "Mr. Punctuality." Jesus' humor in regard to Peter proved prophetic: Peter *did* become a rock.

There are no tools of analysis required by humor in the words of Jesus and situations in the Gospels. What is required is that we recognize and identify humor when we find it. As Trueblood repeatedly asserts in his book on the humor of Christ, it is important that we correct an almost universal belief that Jesus was always serious and that the Gospels are devoid of humor. The humor of Jesus is one of his endearing human traits.

The Rhetoric of Subversion

When we speak of the subversive quality of Jesus' acts and statements, we mean the forceful challenge that he frequently expressed toward conventional ways of thinking. To subvert in this context means to undermine long-established viewpoints that Jesus regarded as wrong. It is beyond the scope of this chapter to get into this subject in detail, so I will be content to name some categories:

- In Jesus' discourses, he sometimes espouses viewpoints that run counter to how people generally live and think. For example, in his discourse against anxiety (Matt. 6:25–34), Jesus commands his listeners not to worry about providing food for themselves and, in fact, "not [to] be anxious about tomorrow." Later in the same Sermon on the Mount, Jesus commands his followers to choose the hard path rather than the easy path (Matt. 7:13–14), something that is counter to our inclination.
- The sayings of Jesus are consistently subversive of conventional ways of thinking: "Blessed are you when others revile you and persecute you and utter all kinds of evil against you falsely on my account" (Matt. 5:11); "whoever would save his life will lose it" (Matt. 16:25).

- Some of Jesus' actions are subversive, as when he broke two taboos at once by initiating conversation with a Samaritan woman (John 4:7).
- Many of Jesus' parables have a subversive element in them, as when help for the wounded man on the road comes from the least likely source, a Samaritan (Luke 10:30–37), or when the bad son is accepted and the dutiful son is rebuked in the parable of the prodigal son (Luke 15:11–32).

As with the rhetoric of the riddle and the rhetoric of humor, the rhetoric of subversion primarily requires us to recognize it, be shocked by it, and obey it. There are no specific rules of interpretation. I noted above that the riddle and humor have each had a somewhat definitive book written on them. There is a corresponding book on the subversive element of Jesus' sayings: Robert C. Tannehill, *The Sword of His Mouth*.[6]

Beatitude

It is an easy transition from the idea of subversion or challenge to conventional thinking to the beatitudes in the Gospels. A beatitude is a pronouncement of blessing, phrased in the formula "blessed is" or "blessed are." The following specimen illustrates the basic form of a beatitude: "Blessed are the meek, for they shall inherit the earth" (Matt. 5:5). The most customary format for a beatitude is a construction consisting of two phrases: the condition that is said to lead to blessedness, and the result or reward of that condition. Nonetheless, it is the pronouncement of blessing that is the essential feature of a beatitude, which does not require the addition of a promise of reward.

---

6   Robert C. Tannehill, *The Sword of His Mouth: Forceful and Imaginative Language in the Synoptic Sayings* (Philadelphia: Fortress Press, 1975).

How major a form is the beatitude in the Gospels? There are approximately thirty beatitudes in the Gospels, some of them duplicated from one Gospel to another. It might seem that a beatitude would not be subversive, but it often is in the Gospels.

To see how this plays out, we need to set the New Testament beatitude against the backdrop of the Old Testament beatitude. The Old Testament beatitude pronounces blessings in this life for the godly and moral person who lives by the norms of God's believing community. "Blessed is the man who fills his quiver with [children]" (Ps. 127:5). "Blessed is the one you choose and bring near, to dwell in your courts [i.e., in the temple]" (Ps. 65:4). Psalm 1 can serve as summary: it pronounces blessing on the godly person, whose reward is that he leads a productive life (v. 3) and prospers "in all that he does" (v. 3).

The beatitudes in the Gospels continue to praise the same character traits and spiritual virtues that are praised in the Old Testament, but the promised rewards are overwhelmingly spiritual and eschatological (to be fulfilled in the life to come). "Blessed are the poor in spirit, for theirs is the kingdom of heaven" (Matt. 5:3). "Blessed are those servants whom the master finds awake when he comes" (Luke 12:37). "Blessed is everyone who will eat bread in the kingdom of God" (Luke 14:15). These apocalyptic beatitudes have an element that challenges the focus on earthly blessing in this life that we find in the Old Testament beatitudes.

Summary

This chapter has been a kaleidoscope of particularized genres and rhetorical forms found in the Gospels. This can serve as a bookend to claims made in the introduction to this guide that the Gospels are mixed-genre books and hybrid forms. Intervening chapters have multiplied the genres and other literary forms found in the Gospels.

Afterword

Jesus Our Hero

The Gospels exist to record and proclaim the acts, character, and teachings of Jesus. At every point in the Gospels we should ask, among other questions, what the passage in front of us tells us about Jesus. I did not belabor this in my guide because I wished not to keep repeating the same point, but here at the end I want to assert that the question of what we learn about Jesus is the continuous question to ask as we read the Gospels.

On November 23, 1879, the Victorian poet Gerard Manley Hopkins preached a sermon at Bedford Leigh in England on the subject of Jesus as the supreme hero. Here are excerpts from the sermon that codify leading points made in this guide:

- "Our Lord Jesus Christ is our hero, a hero all the world wants."
- "You know how books of tales are written that put one man before the reader and . . . call him My Hero or Our Hero. . . . Christ . . . too is the hero of a book or books, of

the divine Gospels."

- "He is an orator and poet, as in His eloquent words and parables appears."
- "He is all the world's hero, the desire of nations. But besides He is the hero of single souls. . . . There met in Jesus Christ all things that can make man lovely and loveable. . . . Make Him your hero now. Take some time to think of Him; praise Him in your hearts."